THE AUTHOR

VERYAN HEAL was born in 1955 and brought up in Devon.
She studied archaeology at Reading University before going
to Cambridge where she researched prehistoric wood
technology. She worked at the National Maritime Museum at
Greenwich and there became Head of Archaeology. In 1987,
she moved to Devon and she now runs a farm and countryside
programme which is involved in the preservation of all rural
aspects of Devon. This is her first book.

BRITAIN'S
MARITIME
HERITAGE

◆

Veryan Heal

First published in Great Britain 1988 by
Conway Maritime Press Ltd
24 Bride Lane, Fleet Street
London EC4Y 8DR

ISBN 0 85177 474 1

Designed by Tony Garrett
Maps by Denys Baker
Typeset by Witwell Ltd, Southport
Printed and bound in Great Britain by
M & A Thomson Litho Ltd, Glasgow

CONTENTS

Foreword

The United Kingdom has a long seafaring history, stretching back to the time before written records were made, into the periods from which only archaeological evidence survives. Long before the famous victories of Drake or Nelson, before the voyages of discovery of the Cabots or Cook, before the Viking invasions, before the building of King Alfred's fleet, even before Caesar's invasion, the occupants of the British Isles were skilled boat builders and seafarers. Prehistoric immigrants and invaders used water transport to reach these shores and to travel, trade and search for food along the inland and coastal waters and across the seas.

As well as wrecking, destruction and wear and tear, time has taken its toll of the vessels which might have survived intact from those distant times, for they were largely built of wood, which decays and disintegrates in most circumstances. Where conditions and chance have allowed them to survive, we can catch a glimpse of the sort of craft which were used, even in the Stone Age; as we move nearer to the present day, where we have written and recognisable artistic records as well as actual remains, that glimpse becomes a more and more detailed picture.

Our maritime heritage is of interest locally, nationally and internationally for social, historical and technological reasons. It tells of the lives of local communities, the skills developed in order to invent and improve designs, the range of activities which water transport permitted and the power and influence at home and abroad gained by mastery of the arts of seafaring.

The preservation and care of the collections and vessels listed in this Guide help us to understand our maritime past; the skill with which the material is presented makes this both fascinating and enjoyable.

Veryan Heal
Chulmleigh, August, 1987

Acknowledgements

Compilation of the Guide has depended on information supplied by the institutions themselves, tourism and museum services, but the presentation of the information is, of course, the author's responsibility. I am most grateful to those who answered my enquiries so fully and to my editor, Jane Weeks, whose inspiration in the solving of problems, and exhortations have brought the project to fruition.

Using the Guide

The entries in this Guide are listed by place, in alphabetical order; there are also indexes by Institution and by Vessel, so the user may consult the listings to discover whether there is a maritime museum or vessel at a particular place, or find the location of a known institution or vessel from the indexes.

Information has been obtained in 1987 and to the best of the author's knowledge is correct at the time of going to press; admission charges are as in 1987 and may be expected to change. Needless to say, vessels, and even museums, may be moved from their present locations. Enquiries to the given address or telephone number should supply the necessary information as to revised whereabouts.

Index of Institutions

Merchant's House Museum, Plymouth.
Merseyside Maritime Museum, Liverpool.
Mevagissey Folk Museum, Mevagissey.
Morwellham Quay, Morwellham.
Museum of Science and Engineering,
 Newcastle-upon-Tyne.

Nairn Fishertown Museum, Nairn.
National Maritime Museum, London.
National Motorboat Museum, Basildon.
National Waterways Museum, Gloucester.
Nautical Museum, Castletown.
HM Naval Base Museum, Devenport.
Newhaven Local and Maritime Museum,
 Newhaven.
Newport Museum and Art Gallery,
 Newport, Gwent.
North Devon Maritime Museum,
 Bideford.

Old Lifeboat House, Poole.
Overbecks Museum and Garden,
 Salcombe.

Paisley Museum and Art Gallery, Paisley.
Penzance Maritime Museum, Penzance.
Peterborough Museum and Art Gallery,
 Peterborough.
Peterhead Arbuthnot Museum, Peterhead.
Plymouth City Museum and Art Gallery,
 Plymouth.
Poole Maritime Museum, Poole.
Portland Museum, Portland.
Priddy's Hard Museum of Naval
 Ordnance, Gosport.

Royal Marines Museum, Southsea.
Royal Museum of Scotland, Edinburgh.
Royal National Lifeboat Museum, Poole.
Royal Naval Museum, Portsmouth.
Royal Navy Submarine Museum,
 Gosport.

Science Museum, London.
Scottish Fisheries Museum, Anstruther.
Scottish Maritime Museum, Irvine.
Shetland Museum, Lerwick.
Shipwreck Heritage Centre, Hastings.
Southampton Hall of Aviation,
 Southampton.
Southampton Maritime Museum,
 Southampton.
South Shields Museum and Art Gallery,
 South Shields.
St Ives Museum, St Ives.
St Katherine's Haven, St Katherine's
 Dock, London.

Stromness Museum, Stromness.
Sunderland Museum and Art Gallery,
 Sunderland.
Swansea Maritime and Industrial
 Museum, Swansea.

Tolbooth Museum, Stonehaven.
Topsham Museum, Topsham.
Torbay Aircraft Museum, Torbay.
Town Docks Museum,
 Kingston-upon-Hull.
Tugnet Icehouse, Spey Bay.

Ulster Folk and Transport Museum,
 Holywood.
Ulster Museum, Belfast.
Union Canal Society Museum,
 Linlithgow.

Valhalla Figurehead Collection, Tresco.

Warrington Museum and Art Gallery,
 Warrington.
Watchet Market House Museum, Watchet.
Waterways Museum, Stoke Bruerne.
Wellholme Gallery, Grimsby.
Welsh Industrial and Maritime Museum,
 Cardiff.
Weymouth Museum, Weymouth.
Whitby Museum, Whitby.
Whitehaven Museum and Art Gallery,
 Whitehaven.
Wick Heritage Centre, Wick, Caithness.
Williamson Art Gallery and Museum,
 Birkenhead.
Windermere Steamboat Museum,
 Windermere.
Woodspring Museum, Weston-Super-Mare.

Zetland Lifeboat Museum, Redcar.

Index of Vessels

HMS *Alliance*, RN Submarine Museum, Gosport.
HMS *Belfast*, London.
Barnabas, Falmouth.
Bertha, Exeter.
Bridlington Lifeboat, Bridlington.

Cambria, Sittingbourne.
HMS *Caroline*, Belfast.
MV *Carrick*, Glasgow.
HMS *Cavalier*, Hebburn.
Cariad, Exeter.
Cheers, Exeter.
Challenge, London.
HMS *Chrysanthemum*, London.
Cutty Sark, London.

De Wadden, Merseyside.
RRS *Discovery*, Dundee.

Edmund Gardner, Merseyside.
Ellen, Falmouth.
Elswick II, Newcastle upon Tyne.

HMS *Foudroyant*, Hartlepool.

HMS *Gannet*, Chatham.
Garlandstone, Morwellham, Tavistock.
Gondola, Coniston Water.
SS *Great Britain*, Bristol.
Gypsy Moth IV, London.

Hero, Exeter.
Holland I, Gosport.
HSL(S) 376, Gosport.

Jolie Brise, Exeter.

Kathleen and May, London.
Keying II, Exeter.
Kindly Light, Cardiff.
PS *Kingswear Castle*, Chatham.

Lively Lady, Portsmouth.
Lydia Eva, London.

Mary Rose, Portsmouth.

No 463, Gosport.

Nore Lightship, London.
Peggy, Newcastle upon Tyne.
Portwey, London.
HMS *President*, London.
Provident, Brixham.

Robin, London.
Reliant, London.

Seagull, Glasgow.
Shamrock, Cotehele.
Softwings, Falmouth.
Spirit of Merseyside, Merseyside.
St Canute, Exeter.
St Denys, Falmouth.

The Three Brothers, Bridlington.
SY *Turbinia*, Newcastle upon Tyne.
Tyne (lifeboat), South Shields

HMS *Unicorn*, Dundee.

Victoria, Linlithgow.
HMS *Victory*, Portsmouth.

HMS *Warrior*, Portsmouth.
PS *Waverley*, Glasgow.
HQS *Wellington*, London.

Zetland (lifeboat), Redcar.

Useful Addresses

Council for Nautical Archaeology, c/o Council for
British Archaeology, 112 Kennington Rd, London
SE11 6RE.   01-582 0494.

Maritime Trust, 16 Ebury St, London SW1W 0LH.
01-730 0096.

Nautical Archaeology Society, Hon. Membership
Secretary, The Riverbank House, River Road, Taplow,
Nr Maidenhead, Bucks SL6 OBG

Society for Nautical Research, 26 Lucastes Road,
Haywards Heath, West Sussex.   0444 453534.

20 40 60 80 100 miles
40 80 120 160 kilometres

Anstruther

Linlithgow
Paisley Edinburgh
Glasgow
Irvine
Bamburgh

Holywood

South Shields
Hebburn
Maryport Hartlepool
Whitehaven Redcar
Coniston Whitby
Water

Castletown Lancaster Bridlington
Fleetwood
Goole
Southport Barton
Liverpool on Humber
Birkenhead
Belan Ellesmere Port
Boston

Cheddleton

Norwich Great
Dudley Peterborough Yarmouth
Lowestoft
Aberystwyth
Stoke Bruerne
Gloucester Colchester

London Basildon
Swansea Newport Southend
Cardiff Bristol Sittingbourne
Weston- Crofton Chatham
Watchet super-Mare
Bridgwater
Arlington Yeovilton Romsey
Bideford Tiverton Southampton Gosport Hastings
Bude Beaulieu Newhaven
Morwellham Exeter Weymouth Southsea Eastbourne
Cotehele Topsham Bembridge
Yelverton Cowes Portsmouth
Plymouth Torbay Poole
St Ives Brixham Portland
Charlestown Dartmouth
Mevagissey Salcombe
Penzance Falmouth
Gweek
Tresco
Scilly Isles, 25 miles
W.S.W. of Lands End

Lerwick

Stromness

Wick

Lossiemouth
Spey Bay
Banff
Nairn   Buckie
Peterhead

Aberdeen
Stonehaven

Dundee

Anstruther

Greenock
Glasgow   Edinburgh
Irvine

Newcastle upon Tyne
Hebburn
Sunderland
Hartlepool

Belfast
Maryport   Middlesborough
Whitehaven

Windermere

Castletown   Barrow   Lancaster
in Furness   Kingston
upon Hull

Liverpool   Grimsby
Warrington

0   20   40   60   80   100 miles
0   40   80   120   160 kilometres

Aberdeen Maritime Museum

Provost Ross's House, Shiprow, Aberdeen, Grampian
Telephone: 0224 585788

Location: Off Union St and Market St, central Aberdeen

Open: Monday to Saturday 1000–1700

Admission charges: None

Facilities: Parking. Shop. National Trust for Scotland shop and audio-visual guide to Trust properties in Grampian.

Facilities for disabled: Access limited to ground floor.

Collection: In 16th-century ship merchant's house. Extensive collection on the fishing industry, fishing boat models, artefacts and paintings including the Harwood watercolours, local shipbuilding, North Boats and North Sea oil and gas.

The Duthie Room, a 19th-century shipowner's office recreated within the Aberdeen Maritime Museum. *Aberdeen Martime Museum*

ABERYSTWYTH

Ceredigion Museum

Coliseum, Terrace Rd, Aberystwyth, Dyfed SY23 2AQ
Telephone: 0970 617911 ext 252

Location: Terrace Rd runs from Marine Terrace to Alexandra Rd (opposite the station), museum on righthand side towards seafront.

Open: Monday to Saturday 1000–1700. Closed Good Friday, Christmas Day to New Year's Day inclusive

Admission charges: None

Facilities: Sales point. Lavatories

Facilities for disabled: Access, lift on request. Lavatories

Collection: Housed in former Music Hall (1905). Builders' models and sailor-made items. Paintings and photographs of sail and steam vessels owned and crewed locally, but operated from Cardiff and Liverpool. Carpenters' and sailmakers' tools. Charts and navigational instruments. Maritime artefacts and ephemera.

HMS Alliance: *see* GOSPORT

Scottish Fisheries Museum

Anstruther Harbour, Anstruther, Fife
Telephone: 0333 310625

Location: Anstruther is 10 miles SSE of St Andrews on the A917

Open: April to October: weekdays 1000–1750, Sunday 1400–1700. November to March: daily except Tuesday 1400–1700

Admission charges: Adult 85p, OAP/child/UB40 35p. Groups adult 35p OAP/child 20p

Facilities: Reference Library. Tea room.

Facilities for disabled: Access restricted due to housing in historic buildings.

Collection: Covers the fishing industry and associated skills. Fishing and ships' gear, models and actual vessels. Vessels include Zulu sailing herring drifter *Research* (1901) and fifie sailing herring drifter *Reaper* (1902) also largest wooden line-fishing craft built in Britain, *Radiation* (1957).

The fifie *Reaper*, FR958,
built in 1902, now fully-
restored by The Scottish
Fisheries Museum,
Anstruther. *The Scottish
Fisheries Museum*

Arlington Court

Arlington, Barnstaple, Devon EX31 4LP
Telephone: 027182 296

Location: National Trust signs from A39 Barnstaple to
Lynton road

Open: April to end October, Sunday to Friday 1100–1800.
Garden and park daily 1100–1800. Last admission 1730

Admission charges: House and carriage collection £2.70.
Garden, grounds and stables £1.50. Pre-arranged parties of 15
or more payers £2 at certain times

Facilities: Parking (300 yds). Shop. Licensed restaurant 1100–
1730. Dogs in grounds only, on lead

Facilities for disabled: Special parking. Lavatories

Collection: Largest private collection of Napoleonic prisoner-
of-war ship models (36) in country. Other late 19th-century
ship models and maritime miscellany. Pictures.

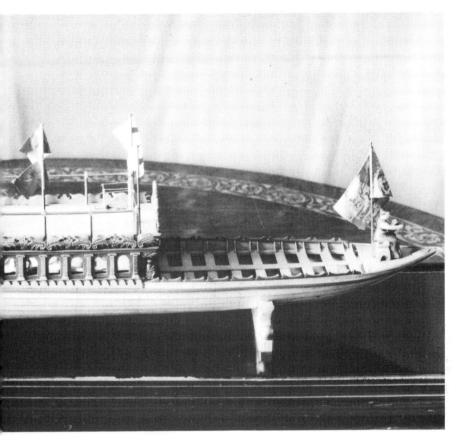

Model of the Stationer's Company State Barge (1820), part of the large model collection at Arlington Court. *National Trust*

Grace Darling Museum

1, Radcliffe Rd, Bamburgh, Northumberland, NE69 7AE
Telephone: 06684 310

Open: Seasonal opening, details from 17 Radcliffe St

Admission charges: None

Facilities: Parking

Facilities for disabled: Access

Collection: Grace Darling memorabilia, including coble used by her.

Banff Museum

High St, Banff, Banffshire
Telephone: 0779 77778 (contact via Peterhead Arbuthnot Museum: see below)

Location: Entry by Library door on High St, museum housed on two floors

Open: June to September, Friday to Wednesday 1400–1720

Admission charges: None

Facilities: Parking. Shop

Facilities for disabled: Access to lower floor only

Collection: Model ships and thematic photographic display on fishing industry.

BARROW-IN-FURNESS

The Furness Museum

Ramsden Square, Barrow-in-Furness, Cumbria LA14 1LL
Telephone: 0229 20600

Location: Follow A590 into Barrow, museum in Ramsden Square

Open: Monday to Wednesday and Friday 1000–1700, Thursday 1000–1300, Saturday 1000–1600. Closed: Sunday, Public Holidays

Admission charges: None

Facilities: Staff will make special arrangements for visiting groups, educational or just general interest

Facilities for disabled: 'Not very accessible'

Collection: Museum housed in same building as County Record Office and Local History Library and can answer a considerable range of local maritime enquiries. Two fine maker's models, HMS *Amphitrite*, armoured cruiser, and battleship HMS *Erin*. Maritime Museum planned for 1988 in Graving Dock.

BARTON-ON-HUMBER

Humber Keel and Sloop Preservation Society

135, Waterside Rd, Barton-on-Humber, South Humberside DN18 5BD
Telephone: 0652 635288

Members welcome to join in maintenance and crewing of the sloop *Amy Howson* and keel *Comrade*.

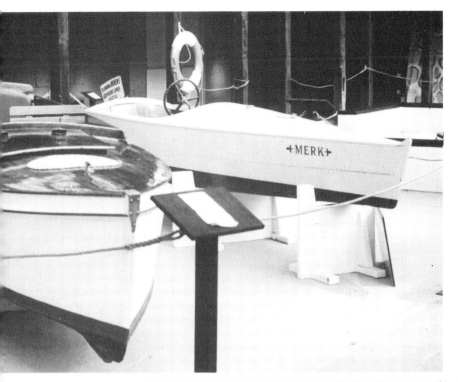

John Andrews' original slipper stern launch *Merk* (1912) and, on the left, an Austin-engined Thames motor launch (*c* 1925), both at the National Motorboat Museum, Basildon. *Kevin Desmond*

National Motorboat Museum

Wat Tyler Country Park, Pitsea, Basildon, Essex, SS16 4UW
Telephone: 0268 550088

Location: By car, take the A13 Southend Road, turning off at the Pitsea roundabout and follow the signposts to Wat Tyler Country Park. By train from Fenchurch Street (nearest underground station Tower Hill), alight at Pitsea, go down the lane, turn left and then walk for ten minutes. By boat, remember that the local Vange Creek dries out at low tide.

Open: Daily 1000–1600

Admission charges: None

Facilities: Car park and cafeteria. Library, archives and video theatre.

Facilities for the disabled: Ramp for wheelchairs

Collection: The museum houses a unique and growing collection of 26 historic motorboats, both for cruising and racing, dating back to *Defender II* (1909) and as recent as *Nordica* (1983). Also contains a collection of maritime outboard and inboard engines dating back to a 3hp Ailsa Craig of 1902.

Buckler's Hard Maritime Museum

Buckler's Hard Village, Beaulieu, Hampshire
Telephone: 059063 203

Location: Beaulieu River, south and east on minor road from Beaulieu

Open: Easter to Spring Bank Holiday 1000–1800; Spring Bank Holiday to September 1000–2100; September to Easter 1000–1630. Closed Christmas Day

Admission charges: Adult £1.50, OAP £1.20, child 90p

Facilities: Parking. Shops, cafeterias, licensed bar, pub, picnic area, and hotel. Cruises on river

Facilities for disabled: Access difficult

Collection: The history of Buckler's Hard as a shipbuilding centre, particularly under Henry Adams. Many ships built for Royal Navy, including HMS *Agamemnon* and others present at Trafalgar. Models, ships' plans, documents. Prints and drawings of ships in action and their commanders. Nelson relics. Francis Chichester's single handed voyages described. 18th-century village life reconstructions.

A half-model of HMS *Illustrious*, a ship built at Buckler's Hard in 1789. *Buckler's Hard*

A 1:200 scale model of Buckler's Hard on Friday 3 June, 1803. *Buckler's Hard*

A view of Buckler's Hard village. The 18th-century cottage interiors have reconstructions of the history of the village.
Buckler's Hard

BELAN

Fort Belan

Isle of Anglesey
18th-century coastal fortress at entrance to Menai Straits,
Anglesey. Information from Merseyside Maritime Museum,
Pier Head, Liverpool L3 1DW
Telephone: 051 709 1551

Collection: The Wynn Collection. Vessels include coracles and
a 1908 steam launch, and gun punt. Belan Dockyard; Belan
maritime miscellany; marine equipment from steam yachts;
ship models, including Navy Board model of HMS *Pike* (1813);
modelmaker demonstrating; nautical instruments, ordnance.

BELFAST

HMS Caroline

Milewater Basin, Belfast

Not open to public but visible.

World War I light cruiser, built Cammell Laird, Birkenhead,
laid down Jan 1914, commissioned Dec 1914. First Light
Cruiser Squadron 1914; 1916 led Fourth Cruiser Squadron at
Jutland. Paid off 1922, RNR depot and training ship since
then.

The Cross of a Knight of Santiago, which belonged to Don Alonso de Leiva, Commander Designate of the Spanish Armada. The cross was recovered from the wreck of the *Girona*, off Lacada Point, Co Antrim, in which Don Alonso perished. The Ulster Museum houses finds from several Armada wrecks. *Ulster Museum*

Ulster Museum

Botanic Gardens, Belfast, BT9 5AB
Telephone: 0232 381251

Location: On south side of city, Stranmillis Rd, close to Queen's University. Botanic Station within walking distance

Open: Weekdays 1000–1700, Saturday 1300–1700, Sunday 1400–1700

Admission charges: None

Facilities: Café. Lavatories. Sales point. Extra facilities for schools by arrangement with education officer

Facilities for disabled: Ramps and chair-lifts. Lecture room equipped for the hard of hearing

Collection: Maritime section mainly material from Spanish Armada (1588), all extant material from three wrecks: *Santa Maria de la Rosa*, wrecked Blasket Sound, Co Kerry; *La Trinidad Valencera*, wrecked Kinnagoe Bay, Co Donegal; *Girona*, wrecked on Lacada Point, Co Antrim. Most significant items: 50lb siege-guns with royal arms of Santiago and Cross of a Knight of Santiago, all from *Girona*. 'Made in Belfast', changing exhibition gallery on local history features, ships and ship-building from autumn 1987.

The Maritime Museum

Bembridge, Isle of Wight
Telephone: 0983 872223/873125

Location: In centre of village, close to harbour. No 8 bus route from Ryde, Shanklin and Sandown

Open: Easter to October, daily 1000-1730, August 1000-2100

Admission charges: Adult £1, OAP 70p, child 60p. Family school and group rates available on application, no charge for teachers or group supervisors

Facilities: Shop. Worksheets for children

Facilities for disabled: Museum upstairs, no special access facilities

Collection: Displays on navigation, shipwrecks and salvage, early diving equipment, deep water sail, paddle steamers, local history, work of Trinity House. Ship models.

Hartland Quay Museum

Hartland Quay, Bideford, Devon
Telephone: 028883 353

Location: Take A39 west from Bideford for approx 10 miles, turn right onto B3248 for Hartland, straight through village. Quay and Museum signed

Open: Whitsun to 30 September, daily 1100-1700

Admission charges: Adult 35p, child 15p

Facilities: Parking. Adjacent hotel with bar, food and accommodation

Facilities for disabled: Museum on first floor with no suitable access

Collection: Small museum, includes history of Hartland beach trade and the Quay (mid-16th century); smack trade since mid 18th century; lime and coal trade with South Wales; lime burning; Hartland Light; Hartland Life Saving Apparatus Co (1892), history and equipment; wrecks in the area since 1641.

North Devon Maritime Museum

Odun House, Appledore, Bideford, Devon EX39 1PT
Telephone: 02372 74852

Location: Right turn at Bideford Old Bridge or at New Bridge onto A386 to Northam. Right turn to Appledore, Odun Rd is first turning on left down main hill into Appledore.

Model of the schooner HMS *Lark*, built for the Admiralty in 1880 by Westacott's shipyard, Barnstaple, in the North Devon Maritime Museum, Bideford. She saw service as an Admiralty survey ship before finishing her career as a cargo vessel. *North Devon Museum Trust*

Open: Easter Saturday to end September, daily 1400–1730, Tuesday to Friday 1100-1300

Admission charges: Adult 75p, OAP 50p, child 10p. Special rates for parties by prior arrangement. Appointments essential for parties and special requests for archive material or guides as staffed by volunteers

Facilities: Free car park opposite. Shop. Interpretation centre (seats 30) with 15-minute audio-visual introduction to area and museum; visitors alerted by bell. GCSE information sheets in preparation, pupils will be able to handle various artefacts. Quiz sheets for children. Growing local archives

Facilities for disabled: Ground floor rooms (3 of 7) and shop accessible. Hands-on material arranged by appointment

Collection: North Devon's maritime past from Viking raids to World War II in dioramas, models and photographs. Models of ships of Vikings to present day. Register of ships trading out of North Devon ports. Large collection of photographs. Special exhibit on steam and motor coasters, working model of ship's steam engine. Exhibit on Lundy Island and its navigational role, working model of South Lighthouse. World War II exhibits on Pluto Coxe and the Panjandrum. Smuggling exhibit.

Williamson Art Gallery and Museum

Slatey Rd, Birkenhead, Wirral L43 4UE
Telephone: 051 652 4177

Location: From M53, take Woodchurch exit on Birkenhead
route. Carry on to Williamson Art Gallery sign on left

Open: Monday to Saturday 1000–1700, Thursday 1000–2100,
Sunday 1400–1700

Admission charges: None. Donation box

Facilities: Parking. Sales point. Education officer

Facilities for disabled: Ramp for access to Art Gallery, gallery on one level only, with easy access from room to room

Collection: Cammell Laird archive photographs (list available). Models of Cammell Laird vessels including *Alabama* and *Mauretania.*

A view of the maritime gallery in the Williamson Art Gallery and Museum, Birkenhead. *Williamson Art Gallery and Museum*

Black Country Museum: *see* DUDLEY

Boston Guildhall

South St, Boston, Lincolnshire
Telephone: 0205 65954

Location: South St, which runs along the east bank of the
Haven, is one way and runs from Market Place to Haven
Bridge. The Guildhall is on the left hand side opposite the
Sam Newsom Music Centre

Open: May to September, Monday to Saturday 0930-1215 and
1315-1700. October to April, Monday to Friday, 0930-1230 and
1330-1630, Saturday 0930-1200

Admission charges: Adult 30p, children up to 16 years free,
but must be accompanied by an adult. Educational and school
parties free. Conducted tours (by appointment only) 50p per
person. Conducted tours outside working hours £5 per party

Facilities: Sales point

Facilities for disabled: None, maritime room is on upper floor

Collection: Guildhall built *c*1450. Maritime room, with fine
exposed cruck roof, houses models, pictures and customs
artefacts associated with Boston's connections with the sea
trade.

SS *Great Britain* in 1987, in
the process of restoration to
her original appearance in
1843. She lies at Bristol in
the dock in which she was
built. SS *Great Britain*
Project Ltd

Admiral Blake Museum

Blake St, Bridgwater TA6 3NB
Telephone: 0278 456127

Location: On A38, in town centre

Open: Daily 1100-1700, except Wednesday 1100-2000, Sunday
1400-1700

Admission charges: None

Facilities: Sales point. Coffee on request

Facilities for disabled: Access to ground floor. Access to other
floors dependent on stairs

Collection: Undergoing renovation, changes likely.
Bridgwater shipping. Admiral Blake memorabilia. Local
history, archaeology, geology.

Bridlington Lifeboat

Lifeboat House, South Marine Drive, Bridlington

Location: On seafront

Visitors welcome to see lifeboat (*Oakley* Class). Attendant or
engineer present. Souvenir shop.

The Three Brothers
Harbour Office, Bridlington, Humberside

The Three Brothers, last of the sailing cobles at Bridlington, built 1912 and used for beam trawling. Restored by Harbour Commissioners. Society for preservation and use (£3 pa). Can be hired for sailing, course within the Bay. Disabled sailors welcome.

BRISTOL
SS Great Britain
Great Western Rd, Gas Ferry Rd, Bristol BS1 6TY
Telephone: 0271 260680

Location: M5, A4, A38, A37 all lead into city close to Cumberland Road. Ship, signposted throughout city, is on south bank of River Avon off Cumberland Rd

Open: Daily. Summer 1000-1800, winter 1000-1700

Admission charges: Adult £1.50, OAP/child (under 16) 70p, children under 5 free. Party reductions, enquire for details

Facilities: Parking. Refreshments. Shop. 12-minute video introduction

Facilities for disabled: None. Limited access to Dock only

SS *Great Britain* designed by Isambard Kingdom Brunel, built and launched at Bristol 1843. First ocean-going propeller driven iron ship. Varied career of 43 years under different rigs, voyaging to America, emigrant trips to Australia, troopship for Crimean War and Indian Mutiny. Abandoned in Falkland Islands 1886. Brought back to Bristol 1970, to dock in which built. SS Great Britain Project Ltd continuing preservation and restoration to original appearance of 1843. Admission desk in Maritime Heritage Centre, where collections of ship models and drawings illustrate 200 years of Bristol shipbuilding.

BRIXHAM
British Fisheries Museum
The Old Market House, The Quay, Brixham, Devon
Telephone: 08045 2861

Location: On the Harbour

Open: July to August, daily 0900-1800. April to June and September to October, Monday to Saturday 0900-1300 & 1400-1700. Limited winter opening, telephone for details

Admission charges: Adult 30p, child free if accompanied by adult, OAP free

Facilities: Tourist Information Centre below museum

Facilities for disabled: Displays on upper floor, chair lift provided, wheelchair available

Collection: Exhibition on British fishing history, changes in methods, history of fishing boats, life of fishermen. Booklet on the history of deep sea fishing available.

BRIXHAM

Brixham Museum and HM Coastguard National Museum

Bolton Cross, Brixham, Devon TQ5 8LZ
Telephone: 08045 6267

Location: In town centre, on A3022 from Paignton and Torquay, next to theatre and market

Open: Easter to mid-October, daily 1000-1730; Sunday closed 1300-1430. Special arrangements: telephone Brixham 2455

Admission charges: Adult 60p, OAP 30p, child 20p. Specially arranged visits and school parties, charges halved

Facilities: Sales point

Facilities for disabled: Access to ground floor only, maritime displays on upper floors

Collection: Ship-building, sail-making, navigation and fishing gear and displays. Brixham trawler models. *Mayflower II* display. Local wrecks and the Torbay lifeboat service. Smuggling. Coastguard National Museum, history of the service.

BUCKIE

Buckie Maritime Museum

Town House West, Cluny Place, Buckie, Moray AB5 1HB
Telephone: 0542 32121

Open: Monday to Friday 1000-2000, Saturday 1000-1200

Admission charges: None

Facilities: Parking. Sales point

Facilities for disabled: Access

Collection: Exhibits on the fishing industry in Buckie, dating back to 1645; herring fishery prosperity in late 19th century and early 20th century. Fish market sheds, ice works, chandlers, sailmakers and yards still building traditional timber boats in the town. Watercolours of town, harbour and fishing villages by Peter Anson.

Buckland Abbey: *see* YELVERTON

Bude-Stratton Historical and Folk Exhibition

The Lower Wharf, Bude, Cornwall EX23 8LG
Telephone: 0288 3576

Location: Take Widemouth Bay Road from Bude, over bridge to Lower Wharf (canal), approx 400yds. Exhibition adjacent to castle

Open: Easter to September, 1100–1700 (1800 high season)

Admission charges: Adult 40p, OAP/child 20p

Facilities: Parking. Cafeteria. Sales, including literature applicable to locality

Facilities for disabled: Access for disabled persons' vehicles

Collection: Figureheads, ship models, wreck artefacts, photographs, canal history, blacksmith's forge, and domestic Victoriana.

Welsh Industrial and Maritime Museum

Bute St, Cardiff
Telephone: 0222 481919

Location: Take Bute St south out of city centre, museum at far end at dockside

Open: Tuesday to Saturday 1000–1700, Sunday 1430–1700. Closed: Monday, Christmas Eve to Boxing Day, New Year's Day, Good Friday and May Day

Admission charges: None

Facilities: Ample free coach and car parking. Bookshop. Video programmes. Activities sheets for children, educational parties welcome

Facilities for disabled: All parts of museum accessible for disabled visitors

Collection: Museum set in Butetown, formerly one of the most extensive ship-owning districts in Britain. Illustration of industrial and maritime growth in Wales during the last two centuries. In Cardiff Shipstores Building the story of Cardiff as a port and the history of its shipowners, in former Ships' Chandlery. Steam tug *Sea Alarm* (1941).

Maritime Trust Vessel
Kindly Light (1904): Bristol Channel sailing pilot cutter

HMS Caroline: *see* BELFAST

MV Carrick: *see* GLASGOW

CASTLETOWN

The Nautical Museum

Castletown, Isle of Man
Telephone: 0624 75522 (Manx Museum)

Location: Bridge St, the continuation of the Umber (north)
Quay of Castletown Harbour

Open: May to September, Monday to Saturday 1000–1300 and
1400–1700, Sunday 1400–1700

Admission charges: Adult 50p, child 10p. School parties at
reduced rate (5p in 1987) if booked in advance through Manx
Museum, Douglas

Facilities: Parking. Sales point

Facilities for disabled: Access difficult

Collection: Primarily the 18th-century schooner-rigged yacht
Peggy (1791), in boathouse (1789), with cabin room above;
facsimile of Nelsonian stern cabin. Remarkable survival of
unique yacht after enclosed dock and entrance to Castletown
Harbour were sealed up, leaving *Peggy* in her boathouse.
Other exhibits include display on nautical life of the Isle of
Man in days of sail; sailmaker's loft; models of fishing boats;
unique nickie's punt *Bonnie Lass*; models of merchant ships;
trading and emigrant voyages; manufacture of ships' biscuits.

HMS Cavalier: *see* HEBBURN

CHARLESTOWN

Charlestown Visitor Centre
(Orbitcatch Ltd)

Charlestown, St Austell, Cornwall PL25 3NJ
Telephone: 0726 73331/2

Location: Take A390, 1½ miles from St Austell, signposted off
roundabout. Cornwall bus and coachways route 25

Open: Easter to October, daily 1000–1800, 1000–2100 in high
season. Last admission 1 hour before closing

Admission charges: Adult £1.90, OAP 95p, child 95p. Family
group discount

Facilities: Parking. Shops. Restaurant, cafeteria, pub. Audio-
visual presentation. Educational packs available

Facilities for disabled: Full facilities

Collection: Shipwreck Centre is part of Visitor Centre. Covers history of west country shipwrecks from 1520 to the present and the varied reasons for loss. History of diving and salvage. Regularly updated. Also local history reconstructions in Charlestown village.

Chatham Historic Dockyard

Chatham Historic Dockyard Trust, Old Pay Office, Church Lane, Chatham Historic Dockyard, Chatham ME4 4TQ. Dockyard in Dock Road
Telephone: 0634 812551

Location: A2 or A229 into Chatham. From large roundabout in Town Centre follow A231 towards Gillingham then signs to Dockyard. By rail: to Chatham then buses from station to Alexandra Gate, Dock Rd, or taxi (5 minutes)

Open: April to October, Wednesday to Sunday and Bank Holidays 1000–1800. November to March, Wednesday, Saturday and Sunday 1000–1630. (Summer and winter times change with changes to and from BST). Last admission 1 hour before closing

Admission charges: Adult guided tour £2.50, unguided £1.50, OAP/child/student £1.50 or £1.00. All children must be accompanied by an adult, children under 5 free, child rate for 5–15 year olds.

Facilities: Parking. Refreshments. Shop. Visitor Centre with audio-visual programme and history of dockyard. Guided tours. Social events. Dockyard Theatre Company. Facilities developing

Facilities for disabled: Car parking and lavatories at Visitor Centre

Collection: Housed in Royal Dockyard which was used as

HMS *Gannet* (1878), a composite auxiliary steam sloop being restored at Chatham. Built at Sheerness, she is the type of vessel enshrined in 'sending a gunboat'. *Chatham Historic Dockyard Trust*

such from Henry VIII to 1984. Principal yard in early 17th century, and built nearly 500 ships including HMS *Victory*. Georgian and Victorian complex; largest concentration of listed buildings in Britain. Museum of dockyard materials, working dry dock, collection of naval ordnance. Working ropery; mast house; mould loft (1753). Unique covered slips (1838–55). Residences including Commissioner's House (1703), the oldest intact naval building in the country.

The Commissioner's House, Chatham Historic Dockyard, built in 1703, is the oldest intact naval building in the country. Chatham Historic Dockyard Trust

Maritime Trust Vessel

HMS *Gannet* (1878), composite auxiliary steam sloop, built Sheerness. Represents transition from wood to iron, with teak hull on iron frames, and from sail to steam, having both sail and steam propulsion. The type of vessel enshrined in 'sending a gunboat'.

CHATHAM

PS Kingswear Castle

Kingswear Castle Excursions Ltd, Chatham Historic Dockyard, Chatham, Kent ME4 4TQ
Telephone: 0634 827648

Owned by Paddle Steamer Preservation Society. Cruises on Medway and Thames. Built 1924, cruised on River Dart. Coal-fired, two-cylinder compound diagonal engine (1904). Members of the PSPS encouraged to help with maintenance and operation.

The 18th-century ropery at Chatham, now in production again and open to the public. Chatham Historic Dockyard Trust

Cheddleton Flint Mill

Leek Rd, Cheddleton, Nr Leek, Staffordshire
Telephone: None for public use. Enquiries: Mr E Royle, 5,
Caroline Crescent, Brown Edge, Stoke-on-Trent

Location: To west of A520 between Leek and junction with
A52. Signposted from road. Access by narrow lane unsuitable
for heavy vehicles

Open: Saturday and Sunday afternoons

Narrow boat *Vienna* (1911), built by Fellows, Morton and
Clayton Ltd, Saltley, Birmingham. Horse-drawn. Bought 1972
and restored 1973-4 by M E Braine, Norton Canes.

HMS Chrysanthemum: *see* LONDON

Colchester and Essex Museum

The Social History Museum, Holy Trinity Church, Trinity
Square, Colchester
Telephone: 0206 712490

Location: Opposite the Library, in Trinity Square, to south of
High Street in central Colchester

Open: April to September, Monday to Saturday 1000-1700,
Sunday 1430-1700. October to March, Monday to Friday
1000-1700, Saturday 1000-1600

Admission charges: Adult 75p, OAP/child/UB40 35p

Facilities: Shop

Facilities for disabled: Ground floor only

Collection: Ship models: oyster dredger *Pyefleet*, lifeboat
Guide of Dunkirk, rear-wheeled paddle steamer *Kitchener*,
hull models from Rowhedge shipyard.

Gondola

Telephone: 053 94 288

Location: On A593, between Ambleside and
Broughton-in-Furness

Sailings: April to October inclusive, from Coniston Pier to
Park-a-Moor

Fares: Adult £2 single, £2.50 return, child £1 single, £1.50
return. Family (two adults plus four children) £8.50. Charters
£150

Gondola (1859), steam yacht restored and run on Coniston Water by National Trust

Unsuitable for disabled; visually handicapped and guide dogs at own risk.

COTEHELE

Shamrock and Quay Museum

Cotehele Quay, St Dominick, Saltash, Cornwall PL12 6TA
Telephone: 0579 50830

Location: A388 out of Saltash, take road for St Dominick, signposts for Cotehele from there

Open: Quay Museum April to October, daily 1100–1600

Admission charges: All visitors 20p

Tamar barge *Shamrock* (1899), built Plymouth, in service until 1950s. Co-owned by National Trust and National Maritime Museum, refitted and lying alongside the Quay. 18th-century office and warehouse contain displays on regional coastal and river trade and local industries. *Shamrock* available for charter in the summer.

COWES

Cowes Branch Library and Maritime Museum

Beckford Rd, Cowes, Isle of Wight, PO31 7SG
Telephone: 0983 293341

Location: Cowes reached by Red Funnel Boat or Hydrofoil from Southampton.

Open: Monday to Friday 0930–1800, Saturday 0930–1630. Closed Bank Holidays and the Saturdays preceding

Admission charges: None

Facilities: Library with 6000 maritime books and old periodicals

Facilities for disabled: Five steps to entrance, otherwise nearly all flat. No special facilities

Collection: Models, paintings and prints of local maritime scene. Photographic collections of J Samuel White and Co Ltd, shipbuilders, and yachting photographs by Kirk of Cowes. Three small craft: Prince Philip's Flying Fifteen *Coweslip*, an Uffa Fox dinghy, and a Tar boat used for fishing.

Crofton Beam Engines

Crofton, Nr Marlborough, Wiltshire
Telephone: 0672 870683

Open and in steam: Telephone for details of steam days. Site
open 1030–1700

Admission charges: Adults £2.00, OAP/child (5 to 15) 50p,
under 5 free

Facilities: Parking, refreshments, picnic area, shop

Facilities for disabled: No special facilities

Collection: Two early Cornish beam engines, 1812 Boulton
and Watt and 1845 Harveys of Hayle. Installed to pump water
to upper level of Kennet and Avon Canal. Oldest working
beam engines in steam in the world. Working models. Narrow
Boat *Jubilee* takes 1½ hour trips from Crofton top lock
through the tunnel on steaming weekends, also private
charters. Details from Crofton Society, 36a Pope Rd, Bromley,
Kent BR2 9QB.

Cutty Sark: *see* LONDON

D

Dartmouth Museum

The Butterwalk, Dartmouth, Devon TQ6 9PZ
Telephone: 08043 2923

Location: From Totnes via A381 or Torbay via A379 and ferry.
Butterwalk in central Dartmouth

Open: Summer 1100–1700. Winter 1415–1600

Admission charges: Adult 30p, child 10p

Facilities: Parking

Facilities for disabled: Museum on first floor of historic
building, not suitable for severely disabled

Collection: Housed in 17th-century merchant's house – built
between 1635 and 1640 – which contains fine panelling and
plaster ceiling. Ship models illustrating development of
vessels from prehistory to 20th century (models of varying
quality). Fine British 18th-century 1:48 scale warship models.
Also *Mayflower*, Brixham trawler, Dart paddle steamer
models. Fine French prisoner-of-war model of two-decker
(wood), fully rigged. Exceptional 19th-century Dartmouth
lifeboat model. Pictures and prints include Luny, C B Hunt.
Large collection of historic photographs and local history
displays.

The Black Country Museum

Tipton Rd, Dudley, West Midlands DY1 4SQ
Telephone: 021 557 9653 or 021 520 8054

Location: On A4037 one mile from Dudley town centre and
adjacent to A4123, three miles from M5 junction 2

Open: Daily 1000–1700, reduced hours in winter. Closed
Christmas Day

Admission charges: Adult £2.40, OAP £1.75, child £1.50

Facilities: Parking, shop, lavatories, refreshments, licensed
bar, restaurant. All booked parties are guided in small groups
with tour tailored to suit their requirements. Excellent printed
Activity Guide for children

Facilities for disabled: Access limited. Lavatories

Collection: Museum laid out as a village, with industrial sites
adjacent, on land formerly mined for coal, ironstone, lime and
clay. Working exhibits on these subjects, 19th-century shops
and pub. Canal St Bridge (1879), cast iron bridge now over
canal cut in 1839 to serve lime kilns. Dudley Canal Tunnel
(1778), limestone mine tunnel 3154 yards long connected to
Stourbridge Canal in 1792. There is no tow path as boats were
worked by 'leggers'. Electric narrowboats take visitors in.
Lifting Bridge (1920), GWR canal/rail interchange from
Tipton. The boat dock is a traditionally-built dock where
restoration and maintenance are carried out, some workshops
built from old boat timbers. *Diamond* (1928), long-distance
horse boat. *Eustace*, railway boat used as spoon dredger.
President, only fully-restored steam motor narrow boat in
country.

Broughty Ferry Castle Museum

Broughty Ferry, Dundee
Telephone: 0382 23141/76121

Location: 4 miles east of city centre

Open: Monday to Thursday & Saturday 1000–1300 & 1400–
1700. July to September also Sunday 1400–1700

Admission charges: None. Booking essential for large groups

Facilities: Shop

Facilities for disabled: Historic building, access limited

Collection: In former estuary fort. Local history including
fishing, the lifeboat, ferries, whaling industry gear and
scrimshaw.

The RRS *Discovery*, built in Dundee for the 1901 Antarctic Expedition, lying in Victoria Dock, Dundee (with HMS *Unicorn* in the background). *RRS Discovery*

RRS Discovery

Dundee Industrial Heritage, Maritime House, 26, East Dock St, Dundee DD1 9HY
Telephone: 0382 201175

The frigate HMS *Unicorn* (1824), lying in Victoria Dock, Dundee. Note her Seppings round stern and unique upper deck roofing, built as a 'mothballing' precaution for a warship built in peacetime. *Unicorn Preservation Society*

Location: On north bank of River Tay, just east of Tay Road Bridge. Follow signs for parking at Victoria Dock. By train, 5 minutes walk from BR Dundee. By bus, 3 minutes walk from Seagate bus station.

Open: June to October daily 1000–1700

Admission charges: Adult £1.50, OAP/UB40/juniors 95p. Dundee Heritage Club Members free

Facilities: Shop, special tours. Arrangements for educational groups on request. Meet the crew. Special exhibitions

Facilities for disabled: Deck levels make access very difficult

RRS *Discovery*, built 1901 by Dundee Shipbuilding Co, for 1901 Antarctic Expedition. Ship's hull was built of massive timber construction to withstand ice-pressure. 'National Antarctic Expedition 1901–04' exhibition by National Maritime Museum in the hold, displays models and illustrations.

HMS Unicorn

The Project Manager, Unicorn Preservation Society, The Frigate Unicorn, Victoria Dock, Dundee
Telephone: 0382 21558

Location: as for RRS *Discovery*

Open: April to October, Sunday to Friday 1000–1700, Saturday 1000–1600

Admission charges: Adult 50p, child 25p

Facilities: Parking, exhibition, shop

Facilities for disabled: Deck levels make access very difficult

HMS *Unicorn*, built Chatham, launched 1824, frigate of 46 guns. Oldest British-built ship afloat and an important example of post-Industrial Revolution constructional ideas: iron knees, diagonal bracing, Seppings' round bow and stern. RNR and RNVR drill ship in Dundee 1873, served as base ship for Senior Naval Officer, Dundee in both World Wars. Upper deck roofing, an original 'mothballing' feature for a ship built in peacetime. Unicorn Preservation Society formed in 1968 and ship handed over to it by Navy. Society aims to restore ship to original condition and the removal of added structures and unsound timber is now under way.

The gun-deck of HMS *Unicorn*, showing a replica 18-pounder gun and iron knee construction. *Unicorn Preservation Society*

East Anglia Maritime Museum: *see* GREAT YARMOUTH

EASTBOURNE

The Lifeboat Museum

Grand Parade, Eastbourne, East Sussex
Telephone: 0323 30717

Location: On the seafront

Open: March to December daily, 0930–dusk

Admission charges: None

Facilities: Sales point

Facilities for disabled: Access difficult

Collection: Housed in former boathouse and displays lifeboats, lifesaving equipment, ships in bottles.

Royal Museum of Scotland

Chambers St, Edinburgh EH1 1JF
Telephone: 031 225 7534

Location: First turning on the right on George IV Bridge as you leave Princes St

Open: Monday to Saturday 1000–1700, Sunday 1400–1700

Admission charges: None

Facilities: Shop, tea room, worksheets for schools

Facilities for disabled: Fully accessible

Collection: Ship models, archaeological, ethnographic, including native Scottish: a sixern, smack, scaffie, fifie, Zulu, and a significant collection of Pacific Island vessels; historical, a series from Viking to recent, including *D'Bataviase Eeuw* (1719); eight Napoleonic prisoner-of-war ship models. Builders' models include Turkish steam frigate *Osman Ghazy* (1864), HMS *Terrible* (1895), HMS *Hermes* (1898), *Empress of Scotland* (1930), whalers *Eclipse* (1867) and *Southern Gem* (1937). Engineering inventors' and builders' models. Model anchors, lighthouse and lifeboat models. Navigational and scientific instruments, including Moorish astrolabe of AD 1026. Marine chronometers.

The Boat Museum

Dockyard Rd, Ellesmere Port, South Wirral LS65 4EF
Telephone: 051 355 5017

Location: By car, adjacent to Junction 9 of M5, 15 minutes from Chester. By train, 5 minutes walk from BR Ellesmere Port. By bus, C3 bus from Chester and Birkenhead

Open: April to October, daily 1000–1700. November to March, Monday to Thursday 1000–1600 (Friday by appointment). Closed Christmas Eve to Boxing Day inclusive

Admission charges: Adult £2.50, OAP/student £1.50, child £1.00. Family ticket £6.00. Boat trips, adult/OAP 90p, child 60p. Boat charter £100 for 3 hours. 10% discount for entrance and non-chartered boat trips for pre-booked parties of 20 or more. Regular user discounts by negotiation. Free entrance for party organisers, free entrance and refreshments for coach drivers

Facilities: Ample free parking for cars and coaches. Party visits can be arranged, also in evenings. Special facilities and work projects for schools. Education centre, conference centre, restaurants and eating room for visitors to eat own food in bad weather. Shop and craft workshops

Facilities for disabled: Most buildings accessible for wheelchairs. Lifts in Island warehouse and education centre

Collection: Sited in Shropshire Union Canal Basin at junction
with River Mersey. Canal originally Ellesmere Canal (Mersey
to Severn), completed 1795 (engineers Jessop and Telford).
Associated buildings include: stables, workshops, slipway,
Toll house, Island warehouse, hydraulic pumping stations,
locks, lighthouse, winged warehouses, company offices and
gauging dock.

Boat collection includes wooden, metal and composite boats
from many fleets; narrow boats and flats; day boats, motors,
tugs, ice breakers, starvationers, box boats and joshers.
Narrow boats (7ft beam) include butties: *Northwich* (1897),
Friendship (1925), *Gifford* (1926) and *Puppis* (1935); motors:
Monarch (1908), *Shad* (1936), *Aries* (1935), *Spey* (1937),
Chiltern (1946) and *Mendip* (1948). Flats (14ft beam) include:
Cedar (19th century), *Mossdale* ex-*Ruby* (1870s), *Scorpio* ex-
Helena (1890), *George, Ethel* (1952), *Bacup* (1954) and *Pluto*.
Tugs include: *Worcester* (1908-12), *Birchills* (1912), *Aleida*
(1939) and *Beeston* (1946). Ice breakers include: *Aspull,
Wappenshall, Marbury* and *Parry II.* Other craft: coal pan
Tom Pudding (1875), Clyde puffer *Basuto* (1901), paddle-
wheeled weed-cutter (1946), packet boat *Cuddington* (1948).

EXETER

Exeter Maritime Museum

The Quay, Exeter, Devon EX2 4AN
Telephone: 0392 58075

Location: 6 minutes walk downhill to west from west main
door of cathedral (signposted). By car, signposted from Exe
Bridge and on all City Centre main routes.

Open: Daily, June to September, 1000-1800, October to May,
1000-1700. Closed Christmas Day and Boxing Day. Evening
visits by arrangement

Admission charges: Adult £2.50, adult party (20+) £2.20; child
(5-15) £1.30; child party (20+) £1.05; OAP party (20+) £1.90;
student £1.30. Teacher with party free. Member of ISCA free.
Other family and group concessions on application

Facilities: Ample parking, ferry between sites, museum shop,
questionnaire for schools. Café, licensed restaurant June-
September and Easter. Snack bar in winter. Pubs,
restaurants, craft shops and 17th-century Customs House
nearby. Some boats for hire

Facilities for disabled: Displays in separate complexes on
several floors, usually without suitable access for disabled,
ferry crossing difficult, though can transfer between sites by
car. Touching exhibits is encouraged

Collection: Working craft and boats of 'exceptional interest'
from all over the world. Visitors are encouraged to go aboard
and explore vessels and their gear. Displayed on three sites on
both banks of the Exe and around the canal basin. The basin
is part of the earliest canal in Britain (1566). Boats are pulled

out along the bank and afloat on the canal and there are two floors of boats in buildings. Portuguese chatas may be hired for rowing on the canal. The oldest pound lock and pub in oldest lock-keeper's cottage 1½ miles along canal. The quay warehouse has four floors of boats, including unique collection of ocean rowing boats while the cellars house the Ellerman Collection of Portuguese working craft.

Extensive collection of more than 100 vessels includes many traditional British working boats from coastal and inland waters, fishing boats from many countries, including the

Exeter Maritime Museum's collection is moored on both banks of the River Exe and in the canal basin, and housed in quayside warehouses and cellars.
Exeter Maritime Museum

extinct Malaysian kolek, an Azores whaleboat, Arab dhows, Maltese, Portuguese, Taiwanese, Hong Kong and Cayman examples. Boats made from logs – dugouts, outriggers, log rafts from Africa, South America, Australia, the Arabian Gulf and the Pacific; reed boats from Lake Titicaca, Kenya, the Mediterranean and the Gulf; skin and canvas boats from Wales, Alaska, Labrador and Ireland; bark canoe from North America; sewn boats from the Pacific and North America; classic rowing boats and sailing dinghies; pilot cutters and steam-powered vessels. Of note: *Jolie Brise* (1913), Le Havre pilot cutter and winner of the Fastnet race in 1925, 1929 and 1930 and of the 1986 Tall Ships Race from Newcastle to Bremerhaven. *Cariad* (1904), built at Bristol, last pilot cutter to work under sail. Others include trolley-launched lifeboat *Bedford* (1896); *Keying II*, Hong Kong junk, sailed around the coast every year; *Bertha* (1884), dredger designed by Brunel, built at Bristol, worked until 1964 and still in steam annually; *St Canute* (1931), steam tug built in Denmark, in full working order and in steam from time to time; *Hero* (1880s), steam launch in working order, used in 'The Onedin Line'; *Ibis* (1905), collapsible metal boat built for Boyd Alexander's expedition from the Niger to Khartoum; *Cygnet* (c1880), rowing boat with swan's neck and head, tender to boat of similar design, a maritime folly; *Three Cheers* (1960s) a Bermudian-rigged racing boat inspired by Pacific proas which came third in the 1969 Trans-Atlantic Race; ocean rowing boat collection – and lots more.

Falmouth Maritime Museum

Bell's Court, Falmouth. Correspondence to Hon Sec Lt Cdr J W Beck RN, Higher Penpol House, Mawnan Smith, Falmouth, Cornwall
Telephone: 0326 250 507

Location: Bell's Court is up an alleyway off Market St, opposite Marks and Spencer. Tug at Custom House Quay in Harbour

Open: Daily, 1000–1600. Museum all year, tug late March to early November. Closed during Christmas holiday

Admission charges: Adult 50p, child 30p, for each site. Reductions for groups, schools and certain bodies. Charges likely to vary from year to year

Facilities: Parking, shop

Facilities for disabled: Access to building. Access to tug difficult

Collection: Maritime history of Cornwall illustrated by ship models, artefacts and displays. Steam tug *St Denys* with unique engine, which worked in Falmouth for over 50 years.

Maritime Trust Vessels
Barnabas: mackerel-driver, relic of Cornish sail fishing fleet, built St Ives 1886, two-masted lugger

Softwings: cutter, used for oyster-dredging, built Penpol 1910

Ellen: Gorran Haven crabber, built Penryn 1882

For details contact Maritime Trust, 16 Ebury St, London SW1W 0LH.

FLEETWOOD

Fleetwood Museum

Dock St, Fleetwood, Lancashire FY7 6AQ
Telephone: 03917 6621

Location: Situated in Dock St overlooking the River Wyre, just
south of corner between Queens Terrace and Dock St. Coaches
to Fleetwood Market set down at door; Blackpool tram
terminus and Knott End Ferry a few minutes walk, head
south along Queens Terrace

Open: Easter to October, open six days a week, 1400–1700. 1
May to 31 October, closed Wednesday. Open Bank Holidays
including Easter weekend

Admission charges: Adult 25p, child 10p

Facilities: Work sheets for younger children

Facilities for disabled: No access

A model of the Royal Yacht
Britannia in the Clyde Room
of the Glasgow Museum of
Transport. *Museum of
Transport*

Collection: Museum of the Fishing Industry with displays
covering Lancashire Fishing Industry on ground floor and
basement. Recreation of trawler bridge, visitors can handle
instruments. Deep sea and inshore fisheries covered. Plans for
display of local inshore boats, including Morecambe bay
Prawner, *Judy*; a mussel boat and a whammel boat.

MV Carrick (formerly City of Adelaide)

Custom House Quay, Glasgow

Location: North shore of River Clyde between Glasgow Bridge and Victoria Bridge

Open: Not open to public, visible from shore

MV *Carrick*, built 1864, Sunderland. Afloat, privately used. Composite clipper, iron frames and wooden planking. Cargo and passenger ship for Devitt and Moore's London to Australia service.

A builder's model in the McLean Museum, Greenock. *George Oliver*

Glasgow Museum of Transport

Moving 1987/8, re-opens 1988 in the Kelvin Hall
Address from 1988: Glasgow District Council Museum of
Transport, Kelvin Hall, 1, Bunhouse Rd, Glasgow G3 8DP.
Enquiries to Glasgow Museums and Art Galleries,
Kelvingrove, Glasgow
Telephone: 041 357 3929

Collection: Fine collection of ship models.

GLASGOW

Seagull Trust

Kirkintilloch, Strathkelvin, Glasgow
Telephone: 041 776 5793 (Jack Hudson)

Cruise on the Forth and Clyde Canal from Kirkintilloch to
Bishopbriggs on converted Clyde passenger ferry, *Seagull.*
Facilities for disabled: Specially adapted for disabled.

GLASGOW

PS Waverley

Waverley Excursions Ltd, Anderston Quay, Glasgow G3
Telephone: 041 221 8152

Operated by Waverley Steam Navigation Co Ltd. Owned by
Paddle Steamer Preservation Society. Cruises on Clyde and
sails from resorts around England and Wales. Details from
address above.

PS *Waverley:* One of the last sea-going paddle steamers in the
world, built for Clyde services in 1946 by A & J Inglis,
Pointhouse, Glasgow. Triple expansion steam engine, double-
ended boiler, originally coal-fired, converted to oil 1957.
Traditional fan-vented paddle box. Members of the PSPS
encouraged to help with maintenance and operation.

GLOUCESTER

The National Waterways Museum

Llanthony Warehouse, Gloucester Docks, Gloucester GL1 2EH
Telephone: 0452 300454

Location: Take junction 12 from M5 or 11 from M4. Llanthony
Warehouse is in docks on east bank of River Severn in city

Open: To open April 1988. For information, telephone British
Waterways Board 01 262 6711

Collection: In Llanthony Warehouse (1873), part of 23 acres of
virtually unaltered dockland. Collection will occupy lower

three floors and will illustrate the story of British Canals from mid-18th century, growth, life, trade and decline. Locks, steam engines, natural history. Canal maintenance yard, blacksmith, woodworking, fender-making and boat painting. Full-scale craft will include: No 4 steam dredger, worked Gloucester and Sharpness Canal 1927–1982, will be working exhibit; BCN tug *Walsall*; wooden river launch *Bluebird* (1924), pleasure boat used on Worcester Avon.

GOOLE

Goole Museum and Art Gallery

Market Square, Carlisle St, Goole, N Humberside DN14 5AA
Telephone: 04045 2187

Location: The Museum is situated inside the library which is a large building beside a roundabout at the end of Boothferry Road

Open: Weekdays 1000–1700, Saturday 0930–1230 & 1400–1600

Admission charges: None

Facilities: Parking

Facilities for disabled: None. The Museum is on the first floor and there is no access for wheelchairs

Collection: Illustration of early history of area formation and development of Goole as a port. Maritime paintings. Temporary exhibitions.

GOSPORT (*see also* PORTSMOUTH)
Ferry to Gosport from Portsmouth Hard. 15 minute service daily 0530–midnight

GOSPORT

HMS Foudroyant

Moved to Hartlepool 1987. Will return to Gosport after refit. Oldest British warship afloat. A sailing frigate of 26 guns, built Bombay with teak hull in 1817 as HMS *Trincomalee*. Renamed *Foudroyant* in 1897. Now a training vessel.

Maritime Trust Vessels
HSL (S) 376 (1944): naval steam launch

Steam Cutter 463 (1899): tender to Royal Yacht

For details contact Maritime Trust, 16, Ebury St, London SW1W 0LH.

Priddy's Hard Museum of Naval Ordnance

Priddy's Hard, Gosport, Hampshire
Telephone: 0705 839766 for information

Location: On Gosport waterfront

Open: Access by appointment only

Collection: Ammunition stores transferred here in 1777 from Square Tower, Portsmouth. Museum housed in magazine.

Royal Navy Submarine Museum and HMS Alliance

RN Submarine Museum, HMS Dolphin, Gosport, Hampshire
PO12 2AB
Telephone: 0705 529217

Location: By train to Portsmouth Harbour Station, regular ferry service to Gosport or special ferry from station pontoon direct to HMS *Alliance*. 12 minute walk from regular ferry, or take No 9 bus. By road: M27 Exit 1, take A32 to Gosport and follow signposts to HMS *Alliance* Submarine Museum, adjacent to Haslar Hospital

Open: Daily, April to October 1000–1630 (last tour), November to March 1000–1530. Closed 24 December–2 January inclusive

Admission charges: Adult £2.00, OAP/child £1.20. Special rates for parties of 12 or more: Adult £1.60, OAP 90p, child 90p (children's educational booklet on confirmation of visit). One teacher to 20 children free

Facilities: Parking. Licensed cafeteria, shop. Information slides and short presentation on loan to teachers on request

Facilities for disabled: Regret only limited access

Collection: HMS *Alliance* 'A' Class submarine (1945) in service condition. HM Submarine No 1 *Holland 1*, Britain's first submarine boat, salvaged 1982 and on view while being refitted. History of Submarine Service from 1776 to present. British, German and Italian midget submarines; full size and scale models. 'World's most comprehensive Submarine Museum' telling the story of how men have lived and fought underwater from the earliest days to the present nuclear age.

HMS *Alliance* (1945) at the
Royal Navy Submarine
Museum, Gosport. *Royal
Navy Submarine Museum*

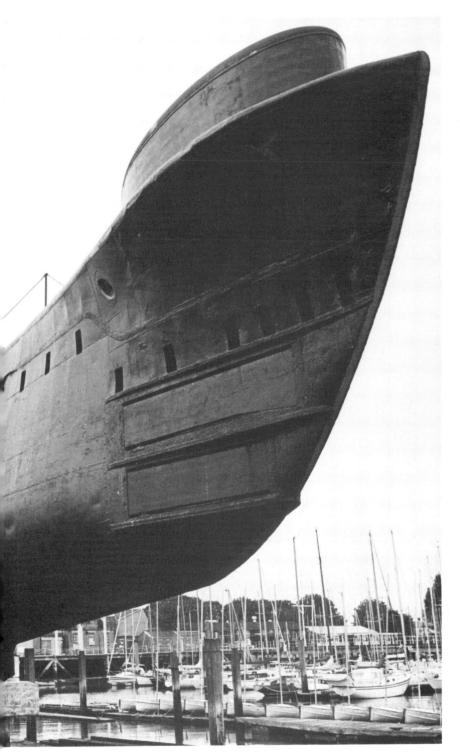

Maritime Museum for East Anglia

Marine Parade, Great Yarmouth, Norfolk NR30 2EN
Telephone: 0493 842267

Location: On seafront

Open: June to September, Sunday to Friday, 1000-1730.
October to May, Monday to Friday 1000-1300 & 1400-1730

Admission charges: June to September: adult 40p, student
20p, child 10p. October to May: adult 20p, student 15p, child
10p

Facilities: Reference library, by appointment. Fully equipped
schoolroom, lessons and guided tours from Museums Teacher
for schools

Facilities for disabled: None

Collection: Boats, including *Maria* (1827), last of the
Broadland racing lateeners. Displays on herring fishery,
merchant, naval shipping, lifesaving and shipbuilding.
Nelson, the Norfolk Broads, naive ship portraits, small
marine engines. Display on Captain Manby (inventor of line-
throwing mortar), ship plans, photographs, maritime
documents and books.

McLean Museum and Art Gallery

9, Union St, Greenock, Strathclyde PA16 8JH
Telephone: 0475 23741

Location: Take Greenock Town Centre turn-off from M8/A8

Open: Monday to Saturday 1000-1200 & 1300-1700

Admission charges: None

Facilities: Tours and parties welcomed, by arrangement

Facilities for disabled: Limited access to ground floor only

Collection: Ship models, engineering exhibitions and marine
pictures including: models of SS *Comet* (1812) (made c1890 by
T Rennie), PS *Iona* (1863), Revenue Cutter; PS *Mona's Isle*,
built for Isle of Man Steam Packet Co 1882; half-model PS
Windsor Castle (1859), first steamer made of iron; SS *Clan
Ross*, MV *Clan Sutherland*; 19th-century Chinese ivory ship
models. Models of steering gear, paddle steamer engine, Caird
and Co trunk engine for naval use. McLean picture collection
includes works by Bone, Boudin, Clark, Daniel, Downie and
Salmon.

Gypsy Moth IV: *see* LONDON

Wellholme Galleries

Wellholm Rd, Great Grimsby, South Humberside DN2 9LP
Telephone: 0472 242000 ext 1385/6

Location: From A180 follow signposts to Freeman St
shopping area and continue straight on until museum visible
at crossroads of Wellholme Rd and Hainton Ave

Open: Tuesday to Saturday 1000–1700. Closed on Public
Holidays

Admission charges: None

Facilities: Slide library and photographic collection available
for borrowing by arrangement with curator. Photograph
copying service

Facilities for disabled: Full access. No adapted lavatory.
Hands-on exhibits can be provided in addition to those on
display, by arrangement with curator

Collection: Napoleonic prisoner-of-war ship models of bone,
ivory and boxwood. 19th- and 20th-century warship and
merchantman models. Comprehensive collection of builder's
models of trawlers covering period 1886–1935; passenger
liners, 19ft builder's model of P&O liner *Narkunda*, and
inshore fishing vessels. Photographs of docks and ships,
ocean going and inland waterway craft. Documents, books
and a wide variety of artefacts relating to the fishing industry
and navigation.

Gweek Quay Maritime Centre

Gweek, Nr Helston, Cornwall
Telephone: 032 622 657

Location: At head of Helford River, B3291 from Penryn

Open: Spring Bank Holiday to mid-September, daily 1000–
1800. Mid–September to Spring Bank Holiday booked groups
only

Admission: Adult £1, child 50p. Schools 50p per child, teachers
free

Facilities: Parking, shop, Café. Five-acre riverside quay. Boat
trips and amphibian rides

Facilities for disabled: Access

Collection: Historic and unusual boats from the Exeter
Maritime Museum Collection. Falmouth quay punt (1897),
lifeboat (1900) last used at Porthleven; dinghy built in
Cornwall by French Resistance and used on raid, gondola,
hovercraft. Boats and ships used in films (videos of films)
including replica of 14th-century Hanseatic cog. Artefacts
from licensed wreck excavations.

H

Hartlepool Maritime Museum

Northgate, Hartlepool, Cleveland
Telephone: 0642 272814

Location: Hartlepool Headland, 2 miles from town centre

Open: Monday to Saturday, 1000–1700. Closed Christmas
Day, Boxing Day, New Year's Day, Good Friday

Admission charges: None

Facilities: Viewing window to contracts under construction at
Fabrication Yard, Fish Quay and Deepwater Basin

Facilities for disabled: Access difficult, collection on first floor

Collection: Historic industries of Hartlepool: William Gray
Collection of ships plans and building records; shipbuilding,
marine engineering (Central Marine Engine Works records),
shipping and fishing. Earliest gas-lit lighthouse lantern.
Reconstruction of fisherman's cottage. Ship models and
simulated ship's bridge.

Fishermen's Museum

Rock-a-Nore Rd, Hastings, East Sussex
Telephone: 0424 424787

Location: On the Stade, seafront, eastern end

Open: May (Spring Bank Holiday) to last Sunday in
September, Monday to Friday 1030–1200 & 1430–1700, Sunday
1430–1700

Admission charges: None

Facilities for disabled: All on one level for access

Collection: Housed in former fishermen's church, alongside
old net sheds. Displays on local fishing, ship models, fishing
nets, old photographs. Includes: Hastings lugger *Enterprise*
(1909), built at Rock-a-Nore; horse capstan, used until 1936;
ship models include 1922 model of *Henri Grace à Dieu* built at
Chatham for Royal Tournament. Note also the net-houses,
'deezes', nearby.

Shipwreck Heritage Centre

Rock-a-Nore Rd, Hastings, East Sussex
Telephone: 0424 437452

Location: Eastern end of seafront

Open: March to May and October daily 1000-1700, June to September 1000-1830

Admission charges: Adult £1, child 50p

Facilities: Shop

Facilities for disabled: Exhibition on ground floor and accessible

Collection: Exhibition '3000 years of Shipwrecks', radar, video, radio. Excellent audio-visual presentation 'Medieval Shipwreck Adventure'.

HEBBURN

HMS *Cavalier*, on River Tyne at former Hawthorne and Lesley Yard, Hebburn, South Tyneside

Owned by South Tyneside Metropolitan District Council. HMS *Cavalier* (1944), World War II 'C' Class destroyer, built by Whites, Cowes. To be restored over next two years. May be open to the public during restoration and will be after. Details from South Tyneside Borough Council, Town Hall, South Shields.

Holland I: *see* GOSPORT, Royal Navy Submarine Museum

HOLYWOOD

Ulster Folk and Transport Museum

Cultra Manor, Holywood, Co Down, Northern Ireland, BT18 0EU
Telephone: 0232 428428

Location: By car: 7 miles from centre of Belfast on the A2 (Belfast-Bangor) road. By bus: Ulsterbus Route 1 (Belfast-Bangor), operating from and to Oxford St Bus Station, Belfast. By train: Selected trains on Belfast-Bangor line stop at Cultra Halt, details from Northern Ireland Railways

Open: January to April & October to December, Monday to Saturday inclusive 1100-1700, Sunday 1400-1700. May to September 1100-1800, Sunday 1400-1700. Easter: check for details

Admission charges: Adult £1, OAP/UB40 50p, child 30p (under 5 free). School parties child 20p, teacher free. Adult organised groups 50p each. Family season tickets £12

Facilities: Guides will give information on each house. Not all exhibits open simultaneously, check in advance. Tea room. Picnics may be eaten in grounds

Facilities for disabled: Part of museum in historic manor, part old buildings in open air setting. Access variable and potentially difficult

Collection: Not much of maritime collection on display. Irish maritime history in terms of the technology of water transport, economic and business history of shipping, fishing and trade, social history and traditions of seafarers and seafaring history. Extensive maritime displays are planned for the future. Check for details. Collection of over 30 vessels includes: steel three-masted topsail schooner *Result* (1892-3), fishing boat *Mary Joseph*, ex-RNLI lifeboat *Sir Samuel Kelly*, Lough Neagh dinghy and a range of vernacular Irish boats.

Hull: *see* KINGSTON-UPON-HULL

Humber Keel and Sloop Preservation Society: *see* BARTON-ON-HUMBER

I

Imperial War Museum: *see* LONDON

IRVINE

Scottish Maritime Museum

Vagrant, a plank-on-edge racing cutter built in 1884, now on display at the Scottish Maritime Museum, Irvine. *Scottish Maritime Museum*

Laird Forge, Gottries Rd, Irvine, Ayrshire KA12 8QE
Telephone: 0294 78283

Location: A78 from Saltcoats or Ayr, A736/737 from Glasgow, A71 from Kilmarnock. Follow directions for Irvine Central, Harbourside, Magnum Leisure Centre. At 132 Harbour St

Open: April to October, daily 1000–1600

Admission charges: Adult 50p, OAP/child 25p, family £1

Facilities: Organised visits, visits by museum staff to schools and organisations with slides, films, artefacts etc

Facilities for disabled: Ramps down to the pontoons, hands-on exhibits, guides

Collection: Ships, artefacts and machinery which hold an important place in maritime history. Local and maritime history. Active boat building, welding, rigging and other restoration work in workshops. Vessels include: *Spartan*, the last surviving Kirkintilloch puffer; *Vagrant* (1884), plank-on-edge racing cutter built by William Fife III at Culzean Ship and Boatbuilding Co, and sailed from pontoon; lifeboats *St Cybi* and *TGB*; yachts; oldest ship the three-masted lugger *Lady Guilford* (1818).

ISLES OF SCILLY

Isles of Scilly Museum

Church St, St Mary's, Isles of Scilly, TR21 0NY
Telephone: 0720 22337. *See also* TRESCO

Location: On main road

Open: Weekdays 1000–1200, 1330–1630 & 1930–2100

Admission charges: Adult 40p, child 10p. School parties free

Facilities: Museum publications

Facilities for disabled: None

Collection: Gig *Klondyke* (1873), used by Revenue Officers. Shipbuilding and seafaring gear, ship models, smuggling tools. Shipwreck material from around the islands including naval stern cannon (1604), breech-loading cannon, coins from HMS *Association* (wrecked 1707). Photographs by the Gibson family of wrecks.

Town Docks Museum

*HULL CITY MUSEUMS
MONUMENT BUILDINGS
PARENT ART GALLERY*

Queen Victoria Square, Hull, ~~North Humberside~~, HU1 ~~3DX~~
Telephone: ~~0482 222737~~ 01482 593902   3RA

Location: In the City Centre, close to Town Hall

Open: Monday to Saturday 1000–1700, Sunday 1330–1630

Admission charges: None

The Spurn lightship, on display in Humber Docks, Kingston-upon-Hull. *Hull City Museums and Art Galleries*

Facilities: Shop, cafeteria. School loans of items from collections. Talks by staff and handling material for schools. Worksheets. Publications. Education room for pre-booked visits. Lunch room for schools.

Facilities for disabled: Collections on several floors, access restricted. Lavatories

Collection: Fishing, whaling, shipbuilding based in Hull. Ship models of local fishing vessels, Humber keels and historic vessels. Artefacts associated with these industries: gear, whale products, scrimshaw. Whaling history, natural history and conservation. Photographs and pictures. Also administering Spurn Lightship, Hull Marina (Humber Dock).

L

Lancaster Maritime Museum

Custom House, St George's Quay, Lancaster, Lancashire LA1 1RB
Telephone: 0524 64637

Location: On west bank of River Lune, through city centre

Open: April to October, daily 1100–1700. November to March, daily 1400–1700. Closed Christmas to New Year

Admission charges: June to September, adult 50p, others 25p. October to May no charges

Facilities: Shop, cafeteria and audio-visual theatre

Facilities for disabled: Historic building, displays on more than one floor

Collection: Housed in fine Custom House (1762–4). History of the port of Lancaster in the 18th century. Displays on Morecambe Bay, the Morecambe gasfield, Lancaster Canal and 'crossing the sands'. Ship models include: *Waterwitch*, 19th-century canal boat (and history of canals in the area); *Thetis* (1804), privateer; several locally made 19th-century models. Display on Morecambe Bay shellfish and wet fish industries includes whammel boat for salmon fishing. Audio-visuals on boatbuilding and fishing.

Shetland Museum

Lower Hillhead, Lerwick, Shetland ZE1 0EL
Telephone: 0595 5057

Location: In the centre of Lerwick

Open: Tuesday, Thursday, Saturday 1000–1700, Monday, Wednesday, Friday 1000–1900. Closed Sunday

Admission charges: None, donations box

Facilities: Tours of exhibits. Staff available to answer questions. Seats available in galleries

Facilities for disabled: Museum upstairs, no suitable access for disabled

Collection: Regional museum including maritime material: a sixareen, a yole, a fourareen. Local and maritime history.

The Old Custom House (1764) on the River Lune, Lancaster, the main building of the Lancaster Maritime Museum. *Lancaster Maritime Museum*

LINLITHGOW

Union Canal Society Museum

Manse Rd Basin, Linlithgow, West Lothian
Telephone: 050 684473

Location: Off M9, junction 3, between Falkirk and Edinburgh. South of Linlithgow town

Open: April to September, Saturday and Sunday 1400–1700

Admission charges: None

Facilities: Sales point

Facilities for disabled: Access

Collection: In former canal stables. Photographs and relics of history of Union Canal, opened 1882, from Lothian St Edinburgh to lock 16, Forth and Clyde Canal.

Victoria

Replica steam packet boat, moored at Linlithgow. Cruises on
the canal
Telephone: 050 844916

Location: as museum

Open: as museum

Fares: Adult 60p, child 30p. School parties, special rates
during the week

Facilities for disabled: Access, but not for wheelchairs.

Merseyside Maritime Museum

'D' Block, Albert Dock, Liverpool L3 4AA
Telephone: 051 709 1551

Open: Daily 1030–1730. Last ticket 1630

Location: By car: Follow signs in Liverpool for Pierhead.
Train: James St Station (Mersey Rail) closed Sunday. Lime St
Station (BR Merseyrail). Bus: MPTE-Crosville to Pierhead;
Ribble-National to Skelhorne St

Admission charges: Adult £1.00, OAP/child/student/UB40
50p, group (20) adult 70p, OAP/child/student 30p. Parking
£1.50, all day, includes admission for driver

Facilities: Coffee shop, water front café, shop, public
telephone, dock cruise, acting performances (Saturdays),
maritime records centre (weekdays), emigration bureau, film
theatre, Maritime Records Centre, demonstrations of crafts.
For schools: school shop, performances by actors, lunch area
(booking required), site activities, quizzes

Facilities for disabled: All access points allow for disabled,
wheelchairs available

Collection: Still expanding into converted premises in 18th-
and 19th-century docks: Canning and Canning Half-Tide
docks, Albert Pier Head and Dock, dry docks, warehouses and
piermaster's house. Particular emphasis on 19th-century and
20th-century merchant shipping and port operations: cargo
handling, pilotage, customs etc.

1000 steam and sailing ship models from the 17th to 20th
century, including Napoleonic Prisoner-of-War ship models,
fishing and coastal craft of late 19th century, warship and
19th-century merchant ship models. Liverpool merchant
companies: T & J Brocklebank, T & J Harrison, Alfred Holt &
Co, Booth S S Co, Bibby Line etc represented in 19th-century
and 20th-century merchant ship model collection (catalogue
available).

Marine paintings include work of 19th-century Liverpool
artists Robert Salmon, Miles and Samuel Walters, Joseph
Heard.

A view of the Merseyside
Maritime Museum,
Liverpool, with Sir Alec
Rose's *Lively Lady* in her
former berth. She has now
been returned to
Portsmouth and is to be
fitted out for sailing.
*Merseyside Maritime
Museum*

Small craft and artefacts relating to ship and boat building industry and allied trades. Demonstrations of skills: cooperage, ship-bottling, etc and re-enactments of dock life, emigration 1830–1930, etc. Small collection of full-size marine engines, working models demonstrating the development of the marine engine from 1837 to 1937.

There are over 30 historic vessels including: Liverpool pilot cutter *Edmund Gardner* (1953); schooner *Spirit of Merseyside* and Dutch schooner *De Wadden* (1917) which traded out of Liverpool; a *Montagu* Whaler; gaff rigged cutter *Sunbeam*; Vietnamese refugee boat; steel ketch *New Liver Bird* (1978); scow, used in graving docks until 1976; Morecambe Bay shrimpers *Daystar* (1894) and *May* (c1920); River Dee salmon boat *Arthur* (1979); Liverpool Class lifeboat *William and Laur* (1949); Mersey ferries.

Also worthwhile, trip on Mersey Ferry, from Pier Head.

HMS *Belfast* (1938), the last survivor of the Royal Navy large cruisers, at her mooring on the River Thames. *Imperial War Museum*

HMS Belfast

Symon's Wharf, Vine Lane, Tooley St, London SE1 2JH
Telephone: 01 407 6434

Cutty Sark (1869), the famous clipper, restored to her original rig, at Cutty Sark Gardens, Greenwich. *Cutty Sark Society*

Location: Moored on south bank of Thames, between London Bridge and Tower Bridge. London Bridge BR and Underground stations nearest. Buses: 10, 15, 42, 44, 47, 48, 70, 78. River boats: ferry between Tower Pier and *Belfast* daily 8 February to 8 November; weekends only 9 November to 7 February

Open: 20 March to 31 October daily 1100–1720 (last admission); 1 November to 19 March daily 1100–1600 (last admission). Closed: New Year's Day, Good Friday, First Monday in May, Christmas Eve, Christmas Day and Boxing Day

Admission charges: Adult £3, OAP/child (5–16) / student/UB40 £1.25. Groups of ten, adult £2.50, others £1.25

Facilities: Education service provides a range of facilities if pre-booked for groups; films, talks, quiz-sheets, packed-lunch room (Tel: ext 126). Shop. Refreshment area

Facilities for disabled: Deck levels restrict access

HMS *Belfast*: last survivor of RN heavy cruisers. Built Harland and Wolff, Belfast. Launched 1938. Damaged 1939, re-entered war 1942. 1943 involved in sinking of *Scharnhorst*. 1944 led bombardment supporting D-Day landings. Flagship in Far East and last fired in anger in Korean War. Trust formed to save from scrap and set up as museum ship to be preserved for nation. Run by Imperial War Museum. Changing exhibitions on board.

HMS Chrysanthemum

Moored on Victoria Embankment, north bank of Thames. Not open to public

Built 1917/8, Armstrong and Whitworth, Newcastle upon Tyne. *Anchusa* Type 'Q' ship. Originally Flower Class Sloop *Saxifrage* and built for World War I convoy escort duty. Owned by RNR, used as drill ship until purchase by Interaction Trust.

Cutty Sark

Cutty Sark Gardens, Greenwich, London SE10
Telephone: 01 858 3445

Location: In dry dock, by Greenwich Pier

Open: Monday to Saturday 1000–1800, Sunday 1200–1800, last tickets 1730

Admission charges: Adult £1.30, child 60p. Groups of 15, adult 80p, child 40p

Facilities: Sales points and exhibitions in hold and 'tween decks

Facilities for disabled: Several deck levels, access restricted. Lift to be installed

Tea clipper, built Dumbarton 1869. Composite construction, iron frames and wooden planking. Built to compete with fastest ships of the time around the Cape to the Far East, but soon outdated by opening of Suez Canal. Ceased tea trade 1877 and then plied wool trade to Australia until 1895. Varied career until 1922, when bought and used as sail-training ship at Falmouth. Moored in Thames until taken over by Cutty Sark Society and returned to original rig.

Gypsy Moth IV

Cutty Sark Gardens, Greenwich, London SE10

Location: On waterfront next to Greenwich pier
Open: April to October, daily

Sailing ketch, built 1966, in which Sir Francis Chichester circumnavigated the world solo, 1966–67. Owned by the Maritime Trust.

Imperial War Museum

Lambeth Rd, London SE1 6HZ
Telephone: 01 735 8922

Open: Monday to Saturday 1000–1700, Sunday 1330–1630

Admission charges: None

Facilities: Shop

Facilities for disabled: Access difficult

Collection: Includes ship models, naval uniforms and ordnance, paintings and photographs. Administers HMS *Belfast*

The three-masted topsail schooner *Kathleen and May* (1900) on display at St May Overy Dock, London.
Teresa Watkins

81

London Maritime Trust Vessels

Kathleen and May: three-masted topsail schooner, built Connah's Quay 1900. Now in St Mary Overy Dock, Southwark, with exhibition on board. Open daily. Details 01 403 3965

Lydia Eva: steam drifter for Yarmouth herring fishery, 1930s. Now in West India Dock. Exhibition in fish hold.

Portwey: coal-fired steam tug used on River Dart, now in West India Dock. Friends of Portwey welcome members' involvement, details c/o 72, Downs Rd, Coulsdon, Surrey CR3 1AF

Robin: steam coaster, built 1890. Now in West India Dock. Details from Maritime Trust, 16 Ebury St, London SW1W 0LH.

A selection of classic wooden boats from the National Maritime Museum's collection at the Wooden Boat Show 1987, held at Greenwich. *National Maritime Museum*

National Maritime Museum

Romney Rd, Greenwich London SE10 9NF
Telephone: 01 858 4422

Location: South bank of Thames a few miles east of central
London. Trains from Charing Cross, London Bridge, Waterloo
East to Maze Hill. Docklands Light Railway: Tower Gateway
to Island Gardens, then foot tunnel under river. River Boats:
from Westminster, Charing Cross or Tower Piers to
Greenwich. Buses: 1, 177, 180, 188, 286 for Greenwich; 53, 54,
75, for Old Royal Observatory. Museum signposted from
station and waterfront

Open: Summer, Monday to Saturday 1000-1800, Sunday 1400-
1800; Winter, Monday to Saturday 1000-1700, Sunday 1400-
1700. Closed: New Year's Day, Good Friday, May Day Bank
Holiday, 24–26 December

Admission charges: Adult combined ticket (main buildings
and Old Royal Observatory) £2.20, OAP/child (7-
16)/student/UB40/registered disabled £1.10. Child under 7
free. Family ticket (two adults and five children) £6.00.
Friends of NMM free. Group bookings (10) 10% discount.
Annual neighbourhood pass (residents of London Boroughs of
Greenwich, Lewisham and Tower Hamlets) free, after
purchase of one normal ticket

Facilities: Book and gift shop and licensed coffee shop.
Research and reference facilities by appointment. Special
exhibitions. Gallery talks, film shows. Planetarium shows.
Photographic sales by order. Royal Park adjacent

Facilities for disabled: Access to parts of museum with
assistance. Wheelchairs available. Warding staff most helpful
with steps etc. Companion of disabled person admitted free.
Lavatories

Collection: Museum in two parts: main buildings house
maritime collections, Old Royal Observatory houses
astronomy and horology. Buildings themselves with the
Royal Naval College form major architectural group with
works by Inigo Jones, Hawksmoor and Wren; in particular
The Queen's House, Palladian style, begun 1619, completed
1635, now undergoing major refurbishment; and The Old
Royal Observatory, Flamsteed House, designed by Wren 1675.
National collections of maritime and astronomical material of
major importance: vessels, models, artefacts, instruments,
documents, books, marine art, some on display, much in
reserve. Re-display programme in progress, some galleries
under re-organisation. Extensive collections, worth several
visits. Range covers maritime archaeology and ethnography,
development of sail and steam, history of Merchant and Royal
Navies from documentary, art historical and artefactual
evidence; history of navigation and position-finding at sea;
rise of Britain as a sea power.

Items of particular note: *Reliant* (1907), paddle tug built South Shields for use on Manchester Ship Canal and at Seaham; hull built into Neptune Hall, paddle wheel and side-lever engine in action and other displays within. Steam launches, including *Donola* (1893). Examples of steam, petrol and diesel engines displayed and explained. Royal Barges, including Queen Mary's shallop (1689) and Prince Frederick's barge (1732), designed by William Kent. Sailing dinghies, including Mirror Dinghy No.1 and other significant designs and numbers. Ship and boat models include major collection

Two 17th-century Navy Board models from the National Maritime Museum collection on display in the Discovery and Seapower Gallery. On the right a ship of 90 guns, a Second-Rate of *c*1675; on the left *St Michael*, a Second-Rate of 90–98 guns built in 1669, one of the earliest models which can be identified as a

of 17th-century Navy Board models used by Board to assess new warship designs, *Cornwallis* (1813), full-scale replica of Ferriby 1 (1500 BC) and Graveney Boat (10th century), ethnographic craft, warships, liners and pleasure vessels. Vast collection of Navy and merchant ship plans.

Collection of swords, firearms and guns for sea service including many fine presentation pieces as well as everyday weapons. Illustration of the development of regulation in the pattern of officers' swords and naval uniforms. Belongings of famous seamen including Nelson's Trafalgar uniform

named ship. *National Maritime Museum*

complete with shot-hole and blood stains; swords of St
Vincent, Collingwood, Cornwallis, Lloyd's Patriotic Fund
Swords.

Navigational and scientific instruments include: 15th-
century astrolabe, compass, lodestones; 16th-century
theodolite by Humphrey Cole (1547); Barberini Collection;
ivory presentation set of navigational instruments by Thomas
Tuttell; Hadley's octants from 1740 to 20th century; Harrison's
timekeepers; chronometers used by Cook and Bligh; early
examples and refined forms of sextant, telescopes, ship's log;
Admiralty Compass Observatory Collection; 20th-century
radio and electronic equipment; astronomical instruments
include armillary spheres, orreries, planetaria dating from
1290 to 1900; an eleven-dial clock by Caspar Buschmann
(1586) incorporating sundials, astrolabe, magnetic compass
etc; sundials, compendia, including one by Humphrey Cole
(1596), hourglasses, nocturnals. The search for Greenwich
Time is traced. Halley's mural quadrants, Bradley's Transit
Room. Airy's Transit Circle Room (which houses the Prime
Meridian), a fully working 28in refracting telescope and the
Greenwich Planetarium are all in the Old Royal Observatory
complex.

Hydrographic collections include charts and atlases: 15th-
century Iberian illuminated vellum, 16th-century Dutch paper
printed, 17th-century English Thames School platts, 17th- and
18th-century French hydrographic survey volumes and charts
from voyages of exploration; 18th-century British charts from
survey and exploration, 19th- and 20th-century Admiralty
charts. Over 230 globes, dating from the 16th century
onwards.

Printed books and manuscripts include official ship's
records, personal journals of seamen and passengers, often
illustrated. Major treatises on shipbuilding, gunnery and
navigation, accounts of voyages of exploration. Public records
of Naval administration, material on the merchant service,
the papers of famous and less famous seamen.

A vast collection of marine art, some of which is used in
historical displays. Special exhibitions run periodically.
Paintings of maritime figures, vessels and actions from the
16th century onwards include the Palmer Collection of 17th-
century Dutch and Flemish paintings, the Ingram Collection
of 17th-century Netherlands School and 18th-century English
paintings. Works by Vroom, Lely, Kneller, De Vlieger, the van
de Veldes, Bakhuizen, Monamy, Chambers, Sailmaker, Scott,
Swaine, Brooking, Reynolds, Romney, Gainsborough, the
Serres, Pocock, Luny, De Loutherbourg, Turner, Huggins,
Stanfield, Cooke, Wyllie, Wilkinson and many others. Prints,
drawings and watercolours only on display occasionally to
avoid deterioration include the van de Veldes, Pocock,
Buttersworth, Wyllie, Everett. An extensive collection of
historic photographs is little displayed, but includes Fox
Talbot, Nautical Photo Agency, Perkins Collection, Gould
Collection and Bedford Lemere Collection.

HMS President

Victoria Embankment, London

The stern and quarter of *The Prince* (1670), one of the extensive collection of ship models at the Science Museum, London. *The Science Museum*

Not open to the public, moored on the north bank of the Thames. Built 1917/18 by Lobnitz and Co, Renfrew. *Anchusa* Type 'Q' Ship, Flower Class sloop, built for World War I convoy escort duty. Previously owned by RNR, London Division, now by Interaction Trust.

Science Museum

Exhibition Rd, London SW7 2DD
Telephone: 01 587 3456

Location: Signposted from South Kensington Underground.
Arrival by car inadvisable, parking very difficult in area

Open: Monday to Saturday 1000-1800, Sunday 1430-1800.
Closed: New Year's Day, Good Friday, May Day Monday,
Christmas Day, Boxing Day

Admission charges: None during normal opening hours *£2.50 now?*

Facilities: Shop, tea bar. Education service. Photographic
order service. Information office. Library (in Imperial College
nearby)

Facilities for disabled: Ramp for ground floor, lifts to other
floors. Notice of parties of disabled visitors appreciated

Collection: Famous collection of ship and boat models of
many periods and places of origin: sailing ships from
Egyptian Pre-Dynastic period to c1700; vessels of war, early
18th century to end of sailing ship era; merchantmen 18th
century onwards, steamships of war, merchant steamers and
motor-ships; European and non-European small craft. Also
actual craft, half models, constructional models. Engines and
turbines and models. Boilers, propellers and auxilliary
machinery.

St Katherine's Haven

St Katherine's Dock, London
Telephone: 01 488 2400

Location: In St Katherine's Dock, north bank of River Thames
just downstream of the Tower of London

Steam tug *Challenge* (1931) and Nore light vessel (1931). Not
open to the public, but visible from quay.

HQS Wellington

Temple Stairs, Victoria Embankment, London WC2R 2PN
Telephone: 01 836 8179

Headquarters of the Honourable Company of Master
Mariners, not open to the public, but access possible via Clerk
to the Honourable Company

Built Devonport Dockyard 1934. *Leith* Class Royal Navy
Sloop, built for World War II convoy escort duty. Last
surviving sloop of 1930s era.

Lossiemouth Fisheries and Community Museum

Pitgaveny St, Lossiemouth, Moray
Telephone: 034 381 3772

Location: A941 from Elgin. On harbourside at north east of town

Open: May to September, Monday to Saturday, 1100–1300 & 1400–1700

Admission charges: Adult 50p, child 25p

Facilities: Shop

Facilities for disabled: Good access. Lavatory

Collection: Fishing heritage of Lossiemouth, models of fishing vessels and graphics.

Lowestoft Maritime Museum

Maritime Museum, Sparrows Nest Park, Whaplode Rd, Lowestoft, Suffolk
Telephone: 0502 61963

Location: A12 to Lowestoft, first turning from the lighthouse

Open: May to September daily, 1000–1700

Admission charges: Adult 30p, OAP/child 15p

Facilities: Shop, with local fishing publications. Organised visits by schools at any time of year, also to docks and fish market (telephone: 0502 65989). School packs on sale. Research facilities by arrangement

Facilities for disabled: Museum on ground floor only. Wheelchair access

Collection: Museum of the Lowestoft and East Suffolk Marine Society. Good collection of fishing boat models: smacks, toshers, drifters, trawlers. Reconstruction of drifter's cabin. Cox collection of east coast lifeboat models and coastguard equipment. Ships' gear, sailors' and fishermens' tools and belongings. Clockwork picture model (1882) of sailing drifter *Jessamine* (LT 22). Prunier Trophy awarded by Mme Prunier, restauranteuse, to skipper for hauling the largest single catch of herring on one night's fishing; last awarded 1966. Marine photographs, Harry Jenkins Collection. Marine paintings, mainly East Anglian artists.

Nearby: Lowestoft High Lighthouse: the first to be built by Trinity House (1609), last replacement 1874. Royal Naval Patrol Service Museum.

Maritime Museum for East Anglia: *see* GREAT YARMOUTH

Maritime Trust

16, Ebury St, London SW1W 0LH
Telephone: 01 730 0096

Barnabas: see FALMOUTH

Blossom: see NEWCASTLE-UPON-TYNE

Cambria: see SITTINGBOURNE

Cutty Sark: see LONDON

Ellen: see FALMOUTH

Elswick II: see NEWCASTLE-UPON-TYNE

HMS *Gannet: see* CHATHAM

HSL(S) 376: *see* GOSPORT

Kathleen and May: see LONDON

Kindly Light: see CARDIFF

Lively Lady: see PORTSMOUTH (in store in Naval Heritage area)

Lydia Eva: see LONDON

Peggy: see NEWCASTLE-UPON-TYNE

Portwey: see LONDON

Provident: see SALCOMBE

Robin: see LONDON

Steam Cutter 463: *see* GOSPORT

Softwing: see FALMOUTH

HMS *Warrior: see* PORTSMOUTH.

MARYPORT

Maritime Museum

1, Shipping Brow, Senhouse St, Maryport, Cumbria CA15 6AB
Telephone: 0900 813738

Location: A595, 596 from Carlisle, A594 from Cockermouth. Through town to harbourside

Open: Monday, Wednesday, Friday 1000–1700; Tuesday, Thursday, Saturday 1000–1300 & 1400–1700; Sunday 1400–1700

Admission charges: None

Facilities: Exhibitions, shop, tourist office

Facilities for disabled: Wheelchair access ground floor only. Displays on several floors

Collection: Illustration of seafaring traditions of Solway Firth with particular reference to Maryport. Port development from small fishing settlement in mid-18th century by Senhouse family for coal exporting. Shipyards from 1765. 19th-century trade with West Indies and South America and Southern Ireland. Post-Napoleonic War shipbuilding, fishing, sailmaking. Later 19th-century iron foundery nearby, and iron steamer building site from where ships were launched, broadside into River Ellen; last ship built 1914. Of note: Thomas Henry Ismay and the White Star Line; Maryport Lifeboat (1865); local pilotage; ship models; half blocks; marine painting.

PRESERVED SHIPS IN THE HARBOUR

Owned by Allerdale District Council: *Chipchase* (1953), harbour tug, built Clelands (Successors) Ltd., Wallsend. Used to tow hopper barges and to assist berthing of colliers at Blyth and Seaham. To Maryport 1983
Vic 96 (1945), steam lighter, built Richard Dunston Ltd, Thorne, Humberside. As *C668*, based at Sheerness. To Maryport 1971
Harecraig II (1951), steam tug, built Ferguson and Son, Port Glasgow. Originally *Flying Buzzard*, overrun and sunk, recovered, used on River Tay. To Maryport 1983.

Owned by Maryport Steamship Company: *Scharhörn* (1908) steam yacht, built Jansen and Schmilinski & Co, Hamburg. State yacht for Burgomeisters. Survey vessel under Third Reich. Acquired by Maryport Steamship Company after private ownership.

Emily Barratt (1912) trading schooner (only English example still afloat), built for Hodbarrow Mining Co, Millom. Irish Sea and then Welsh coal trade. Barrage balloon barge 1940, 1944 port duties, 1945 classed as constructive total loss. 1948 refitted as ketch, sank at moorings 1982. Restored and brought to Maryport.

Mary Rose: *see* PORTSMOUTH

MEVAGISSEY

Mevagissey Folk Museum

East Quay, Mevagissey, Cornwall
Telephone: 0726 843568

Location: B3273 from St Austell to Mevagissey, follow signs for Quay from village.

Open: Easter to end of September, Monday to Saturday 1100–1700, Sunday 1300–1700

Admission charges: Adult 20p, OAP/child 10p

Facilities: Sales point

Facilities for disabled: Access to ground floor only

Collection: Fishing, farming and local history.

Captain Cook Birthplace Museum

Stewart Park, Marton, Middlesborough, Cleveland
Telephone: 0642 311211

Location: Turn east of A19 onto A174, then north onto A172, from where museum well signposted. By bus: local bus stops at Marton Station, close by

Open: Summer 1000–1800, winter 0900–dusk. Last tickets 45 minutes before closing

Admission charges: Adult 30p, OAP/child 10p

Facilities: Parking, shop, café

Facilities for disabled: Good access: ramp or lift access to all areas

Collection: The life of Captain Cook, illustrated with models and relics.

MORWELLHAM

Morwellham Quay

Tavistock, Devon, PL19 8JL
Telephone: 0822 832766

Location: Off A390, 2 miles west of Tavistock, clearly signposted

Open: Summer 1000–1730 (last admission 1600), winter 1000–1630 (last admission 1430)

Admission charges: Adult £3.95, OAP/student £2.95, child £2.45. Party rates: adult £2.85, OAP/student £2.35, child £1.70

Facilities: Introductory slide-show, shops, tea room. In summer, pasty house

Facilities for disabled: Parts of site unsuitable for wheelchairs. Lavatories

Collection: Ancient port on the River Tamar, greatest copper port in the Victorian Empire. Reconstructed as in 1868, crafts and ports activities re-enacted. *Garlandstone* (1909) trading ketch, last ship to be built on the Tamar at James Goss' shipyard, Calstock.

N

Nairn Fishertown Museum

Laing Hall, King St, Nairn, Highland IV12 4PP
Telephone: 0667 53331

Location: A96 from Elgin or Inverness, A939 from Grantown-on-Spey

Open: May to September Tuesday, Thursday and Saturday 1430-1630; Monday, Wednesday and Friday 1830-2030

Admission charges: Adult 10p, child 5p. Group rates on application

Facilities: Parking

Facilities for disabled: Access

Collection: Photographs and articles connected with the Moray Firth and herring fishing industries during the steam drifter era. Exhibits on domestic life in the fishertown.

National Maritime Museum: *see* LONDON

Gondola: *see* CONISTON WATER

National Waterways Museum: *see* GLOUCESTER

NEWCASTLE-UPON-TYNE

Museum of Science and Engineering

Blandford House, Blandford Square, Newcastle-upon-Tyne, NE1 4JA
Telephone: 091 2326789

Location: Take A69 into Newcastle; in Westgate Rd turn right into Blandford St, museum at far end

Open: Tuesday to Friday 1000-1730, Saturday 1000-1630. Closed Sunday and Monday

Admission charges: None

Facilities: Museum shop, cafeteria. Education worksheets

Facilities for disabled: Lift entrance. Wheelchairs available

Collection: Permanent maritime gallery; strongest theme is development and diversity of steam merchant ship 1880-1930. 150 builders' models of Tyneside ships including first successful steam colliers, *John Bowes* (1852) and oil tankers, *Gluckshauf* (1885); Armstrong and Whitworth 1882-1905; Robert Thompson sailing vessel half models: exceptional models of RMS *Mauretania* (1907) and HMS *Nelson* (1927). Tyne and Wearside builders' ship plans and photographs, including prototype of World War II Liberty ships, SS *Empire Liberty*. Bone and wood miniature models of 18th- and 19th-century warships, French prisoner-of-war ship models and recent ones by Donald Ash. Marine painting, marine engineering; navigational instruments; marine engine models; regional lifesaving craft models; British and foreign small craft models.

Vessels: *Blossom:* northeast coast fishing mule, owned by the Maritime Trust. *Glad Tidings* BK 10 (1929), motor/sail coble, 1929. *Elswick No 2:* Tyne wherry (1930s), owned by the Maritime Trust.

Exhibits in the Marine Gallery, Museum of Science and Engineering, Newcastle-upon-Tyne. *Newcastle Museum of Science and Engineering*

Newhaven Local and Maritime Museum

West Foreshore, Newhaven, East Sussex
Telephone: 0273 514760

Location: Western end of foreshore

Open: Easter to 31 October Saturday, Sunday and Bank Holiday Monday 1430–1800

Admission charges: Adult 15p, child free

Facilities: Sales point

Facilities for disabled: Access

Collection: Display and collection of photographs of Newhaven, Seaford and the area. History of cross-channel ferries. Possibly moving to The Fort in 1988, this signposted.

NEWPORT

Newport Museum and Art Gallery

John Frost Square, Newport, Gwent NP9 1HZ
Telephone: 0633 840064

Location: Junction 26 from M4, in pedestrian area in town centre

Open: Monday to Thursday 0930–1700, Friday 0900–1630, Saturday 0930–1600

Admission charges: None

Facilities: Parking near. Shop

Facilities for disabled: Access

Collection: Artefacts reflecting the development of this important port. Professional models and half models of coaster, tramp, clipper, steamers and good local models. Relics and ephemera of maritime Newport. Records of Newport Pilotage Authority, Newport Harbour Commission and Lloyds Shipping Register 1845 to the present. Transporter bridge drawings and scale model. Photographs of port and shipping.

NORWICH

Bridewell Museum of Norwich Trades and Industries

Bridewell Alley, St Andrew's St, Norwich, Norfolk NR2 1AQ
Telephone: 0603 611277 ext 298. Weekends 623701

Location: City Centre, St Andrew's St runs east to west, north of the castle and south of the river. Bridewell Alley runs south off St Andrew's St at St Andrew's church

Open: 1000–1700

Admission charges: Summer: adult 40p, student 20p, child 10p. Winter: adult 20p, student 15p, child 10p

Facilities: Lessons given to parties of school children, booking essential (ext 282)

Facilities for disabled: None. Museum on confined site, building mediaeval and later on several floors with many stairs

Collection: River craft models: keel, wherry, Norfolk punt, trading wherry converted to a pleasure wherry.

Paisley Museum and Art Gallery

High St, Paisley, Renfrewshire, PA1 2BA
Telephone: 041 889 3151

Location: From M8 motorway take any road signposted for Paisley Town Centre. Museum at the western end of the main shopping centre

Open: Monday to Saturday 1000–1700. (No professional staff in attendance on Saturday)

Admission charges: None

Facilities: Sales point. Education officer provides organised projects for pre-booked school parties

Facilities for disabled: Access severely limited. Stairway access to each of seven exhibition areas. Easy access to some areas only

Collection: Archive material relating to Fleming & Ferguson. Photographs and yard models from Simons and Lobnitz. Both had local yards specialising in dredger building. Shipyard models from other local firms.

Penzance Maritime Museum

19, Chapel St, Penzance, Cornwall TR18 4AF (November to April, mail to be sent to 52, Chapel St)
Telephone: 0736 63324

Location: Turn left at the top of Penzance main street

Open: Monday to Saturday 1000–1700

Admission charges: Adult £1, OAP/child 60p. Discount for schools

Facilities for disabled: Not suitable, as access is difficult

Collection: Finds from wrecks displayed in galleries built as a 4-decked man-o'-war.

PETERBOROUGH

Peterborough Museum and Art Gallery

Priestgate, Peterborough PE1 1LF
Telephone: 0733 43329

Location: Priestgate is off Bourges Boulevard, part of the
inner ring road, between its junctions with the A1 and A15

Open: May to 30 September, Tuesday to Saturday and Bank
Holiday Mondays 1000-1700; October to April, Tuesday to
Friday 1200-1700, Saturday 1000-1700. Closed: Christmas
Day, Boxing Day, Good Friday

Admission charges: None

Facilities: Parking nearby

Facilities for disabled: Limited access, contact curator in
advance if possible

Collection: Fine collection of bone prisoner-of-war models from
Napoleonic War period, made by prisoners in Norman Cross
PoW prison. Also Chinese junk model and British first-rater of
Napoleonic War. Ten models in all.

PETERHEAD

Peterhead Arbuthnot Museum

St Peter St, Peterhead, Aberdeenshire AB4 6QD
Telephone: 0779 77778

Location: In library building at junction of St Peter St and
Queen St

Open: Monday to Saturday 1000-1200, 1400-1700

Admission charges: None

Facilities: Parking, shop

Facilities for disabled: No access

Collection: Models showing development of fishing boat from
sail to diesel. Relics of sailing ships trading out of Peterhead.
Whaling industry represented by model ships and relics of
whalers, also arctic animals and Eskimo artefacts.

PLYMOUTH

Plymouth City Museum and Art Gallery

Drake Circus, Plymouth, Devon PL4 8AJ
Telephone: 0752 668000 ext 4878

Location: In city centre, Drake Circus is at the junction of
Coburg St and Charles St, museum at the south end of Drake
Circus

Open: Monday to Friday 1000-1730; Saturday 1000-1700

Admission charges: None

Facilities: Shop. Access to marine paintings by appointment only

Facilities for disabled: Rear access for disabled

Collection: Marine paintings and prints. Ship models, including French Prisoner-of-War bone models. Some ship equipment.

Elizabethan House

32, New St, Plymouth, PL1 2NA
Telephone: as above, ext 4280

Location: New St is between Citadel St and the Barbican, off the north east corner of the Hoe

Open: As for Merchant's House Museum, closing at 1630 in winter

Admission charges: Adult 25p, child 10p. Free for pre-booked educational parties

Facilities: Sales point

Facilities for disabled: Access restricted, historic building

Collection: Elizabethan house as would have been occupied by sea captain.

HM Naval Base Museum, Devonport

South Yard (PC 1422), Devonport, Plymouth PL1 4SG
Telephone: 0752 552611

Location: Naval Base well signposted from city centre

Open: 0730–1145 & 1230–1700. Flexible times for visitors. Visitors must be in groups of 10–25

Admission charges: None

Facialities: Special arrangements for schools. Conducted tours, historical and modern

Facilities for disabled: Variable access

Collection: General naval memorabilia, historic and modern.

Merchant's House Museum

33 St Andrews St, Plymouth
Telephone: as above, ext 4383

Location: In the city centre, north off the east end of Notte St

Open: Monday to Friday 1000–1300 & 1415–1730; Saturday 1000–1300 & 1415–1700

Admission charges: Adult 25p, child 10p. Free for pre-booked educational parties

Facilities: Sales point

Facilities for disabled: Access severely restricted

Collection: Local social history including one room on the life of the sailor.

see also YELVERTON (Buckland Abbey)

POOLE

Old Lifeboat House

East Quay, Poole, Dorset
Telephone: 0202 671133

Location: On quay, eastern end

Open: Easter to 30 September, daily 1015–1230 & 1430–1730. Visits during outside hours by arrangement with RNLI at above telephone number

Admission charges: None. Collection box for RNLI

Facilities: Shop

Facilities for disabled: No special facilities, ground floor display access possible

Collection: Former Poole lifeboat *Thomas Kirk Wright* and associated material.

The lifeboat *Worcester Cadet* and her crew, Brightstone Grange, Isle of Wight. The photograph was taken between 1880 and 1888. *Royal National Lifeboat Institution*

Poole Maritime Museum

Paradise St, The Quay, Poole, Dorset
Telephone: 0202 675151 ext 3559

Location: On the quay

Open: Monday to Saturday 1000–1700; Sunday 1400–1700.
Closed Good Friday, Christmas Day, Boxing Day

Admission charges: Adult 45p, child 25p

Facilities: Shop

Facilities for disabled: Access difficult

Collection: In 15th-century former port warehouse. Mainly local maritime history, models and full size craft including Iron Age logboat; X Class yacht (1909); International 14 dinghy. Displays on smuggling, Spanish Armada and Newfoundland trade.

The interior of Poole Maritime Museum. *Poole Maritime Museum*

Royal National Lifeboat Museum

RNLI Headquarters, West Quay Road, Poole, Dorset
Telephone: 0202 671133

Location: On the quay, western end

Open: Monday to Friday 0930-1630. Closed Bank Holidays

Admission charges: None

Facilities: Free parking

Facialities for disabled: Access involves one step, display all
on ground floor

Collection: Displays on development and history of RNLI,
lifeboats and lifesaving since 1824. Models, paintings and
artefacts.

The only known
contemporary
representation of Henry
VIII's *Mary Rose*, a
watercolour in the margin of
the Anthony Role, an
inventory of the King's Ships
published in 1546.
*Magdalene College,
Cambridge*

PORTLAND

The Portland Museum

217 Wakeham, Portland, Dorset DT5 1HS
Telephone: 0305 821804

Location: On main A354 road to Portland Bill

Open: May to September, daily 1000–1730, Sunday 1100–1700.
Winter, Tuesday to Saturday 1000–1300, & 1400–1700. Closed
Sunday and Monday.

Admission charges: Adult 65p, OAP 30p, students and
children free

Facilities: Museum displays

Facilities for disabled: Wheelchair access difficult; narrow
doorways; no special provisions

Collection: History of the Isle of Portland, one section devoted
to maritime relics. Pictorial display of local shipwrecks.

PORTSMOUTH

Navy Days: Usually August Bank Holiday weekend;
telephone for details on 0705 839766. RN ships open to public,
displays etc.

PORTSMOUTH

D-Day Museum

Clarence Esplanade, Portsmouth PO5 3NT
Telephone: 0705 827261

Location: On the front

Open: Daily 1030–1730. Closed Christmas Eve, Christmas
Day, Boxing Day

Admission charges: Adult £1.50, OAP/child/student £1.00

Facilities: Parking and shop. Multi-lingual presentation

Facilities for disabled: Full facilities

Collection: Overlord embroidery, multi-lingual audio-visual
show, photographs, maps, models, equipment and vehicles.

PORTSMOUTH

Mary Rose Ship Hall and Exhibition

College Rd, HM Naval Base, Portsmouth, Hants PO1 3LX
Telephone: 0705 750521

Location: By road: follow signposting from M275 into
Portsmouth. No vehicle access to Base. By train, coach or
ferry: alight at Portsmouth Harbour Station interchange.
Enter Naval Base by Victory Gate

Open: March to 31 October 1030-1730; 1 November to 1 March 1030-1700. Closed Christmas Day. Last tickets one hour before closing

Admission charges: Low season (until April and from 1 October): Adult £2.50, OAP/child £1.50, family £6.50. High season (1 May to 30 September) Adult £2.80, OAP/child £1.80, family £7.50. Group rates and special arrangements: contact Mary Rose Trust at address above

Facilities: Shop with wide range of *Mary Rose* souvenirs

Facilities for disabled: Exhibition fully accessible for wheelchairs, access to Ship Hall restricted to upper viewing gallery

Collection: Henry VIII's warship *Mary Rose*, built at Portsmouth 1509-10, rebuilt 1536, sank in Solent 1545 as she set out against the French. After location and excavation, raised in 1982 and transferred to a dry dock, now the Ship Hall, where reconstruction and conservation are in progress.

Exhibition, in Georgian timber boathouse, displays finds from the excavation and reconstructions of parts of the ship. The wreck preserved the ship's gear and the personal belongings of those on board on 19 July 1545, providing a unique group of material including items unknown from elsewhere. Ranges from guns and parts of the rigging, to musical instruments, games and clothing, as well as plant remains, seeds, a flea and barber-surgeon's medical chest, giving insight into health of the crew and conditions on board. Excellent audio-visual presentation on the history of the ship, the excavation and recovery.

A bronze gun recovered from the wreck of the *Mary Rose* in 1979, on display in the Mary Rose Exhibition, Portsmouth. In the background is a reconstruction of the gun-decks of the *Mary Rose*. *Mary Rose Trust*

Royal Naval Museum

HM Naval Base, Portsmouth, Hampshire PO1 3LR
Telephone: 0705 822351 ext 2368/9 or 0705 733060

Location: To Naval Base as for *Mary Rose*, then follow signs

Open: Daily 1030-1700, some seasonal variations

Admission charges: Adult 50p, OAP/child 25p, family £1.25.
Parties, one person in ten admitted free

Facilities: No parking in base but public car parks close to
Base. Large shop for HMS *Victory* and RN souvenirs. Student
packs. Buffet (soup, cold snacks, drinks). Library and
archives, by appointment only open 1000-1230 & 1400-1600

Facilities for disabled: All galleries accessible for wheelchairs.
Lavatory facilities. Cars may be brought to the Museum door
by prior arrangement

A view of the Royal Naval
Museum, Portsmouth, which
is housed in three Georgian
dockyard storehouses.
Royal Naval Museum

Collection: Housed in three Georgian storehouses, deals with
the entire history of the Royal Navy from Tudor times to the
South Atlantic Campaign of 1982. Main exhibitions: Rise of
Royal Navy 1485-1792; HMS *Victory*; Wyllie panorama of

Trafalgar, Nelson and Lady Hamilton; heyday of fighting sail (1793–1815); end of the sailing Navy (1816–1860); Victorian heyday (1861–1905); twentieth century; modern Navy. These illustrated by models, relics, documents, paintings, belongings and audio-visuals. Also Lambert-McCarthy Collection of Nelsoniana; Douglas-Morris Collection of medals; Ferrers-Walker Collection of ship relics. Society of Friends can be contacted through museum.

PORTSMOUTH

HMS Victory

The Commanding Officer, HMS Victory, HM Naval Base, Portsmouth PO1 3PZ
Telephone: 0705 839766 (Naval Heritage Visits)

Location: as for *Mary Rose*, follow signs inside Base

Open: March to October, Monday to Saturday 1030–1730, Sunday 1300–1700; November to February, Monday to Saturday 1030–1630, Sunday 1300–1630. Closed Christmas Day

Admission charges: Adult £1.80, OAP/child £1. 10% discount for parties booked in advance

Facilities: Shop

Facilities for disabled: Access to decks difficult

HMS *Victory*, laid down Chatham 1759, the oldest surviving ship of the line of battle, Nelson's flagship at Trafalgar (1805). Now flagship of Commander-in-Chief, Naval Home Command. Has been in continuous commission since 1778. Now undergoing most extensive refit since 1922.

PORTSMOUTH

HMS Warrior

Victory Gate, HM Naval Base, Portsmouth PO1 3QX
Telephone: 0705 291379

Location: as for *Mary Rose*, ship clearly visible from the Hard

Open: Winter, daily, 1030–1700; summer daily 1030–1730

Admission charges: Adult £3.00, child (5–16) £1.50. No concessions at present, under consideration

Facilities: Pre-booked groups

Facilities for disabled: No provisions made as restoration is faithful to 1851/1864 period

HMS *Warrior*, built on Thames at Blackwell 1860, first iron-built, armoured sea-going warship. Iron hull, wrought iron 4½in thick backed by 18in of teak. Largest, fastest, best-protected warship of her time.

HMS President: *see* LONDON

HMS *Victory* (1759), the oldest surviving ship of the line of battle and Nelson's flagship at Trafalgar (1805), has been in continuous commission since 1778. She lies at Portsmouth as flagship of the Commander-in-Chief, Naval Home Command. *HMS Victory*

R

Zetland Lifeboat Museum

5, King St, Redcar, Cleveland
Telephone: No public telephone

Location: A174 from Whitby or outskirts of Middlesborough, A1042 into Redcar. On promenade, overlooking the beach

Open: May to September, daily 1100–1600

Admission charges: No charge, donation boxes

Facilities: School parties by arrangement (0642 485370), storyteller provided

Facilaities for disabled: Access to boathouse and ground floor gallery

Collection: The boathouse (1877) specifically built to house a lifeboat, with a reading room above for local fishermen and living accommodation for coxwain. Lifeboat *Zetland* (1800), built by Henry Greathead, oldest in the world.

Romsey

Broadlands

Romsey, Hampshire
Telephone: 0794 516878

Location: Off A31 south of Romsey. Half-hourly bus service from Southampton, hourly from Winchester. BR station

Open: April to September, Tuesday to Sunday 1000–1700, Mondays in August and September and Bank Holidays

Admission charges: Adult £3.20, reduced rates for OAP/child/disabled. Details on request

Facilities: House (18th century) and riverside lawns. Shop.

Facilities for disabled: Access restricted in historic building

Collection: Exhibition of life of Lord Mountbatten, audio-visual presented by him. Uniforms, medals, HMS *Kelly* Corridor.

Royal Marines Museum: *see* SOUTHSEA

Royal Naval Museum: *see* PORTSMOUTH

Royal Navy Museum and HMS Alliance: *see* GOSPORT

Island Cruising Club

Island St, Salcombe, Devon

Not a museum, but looks after preserved ships *Hoshi* (1908), two-masted schooner, built Camper and Nicholson, and *Provident* (1924), ketch-rigged former Brixham Trawler, being refitted and owned by the Maritime Trust.

Overbecks, Museum and Garden

Sharpitor, Salcombe, Devon TQ8 8LW
Telephone: 054884 2893

Location: Signposted from A381 at Marlborough, just north of Salcombe

Open: 1 April (or Easter if earlier) to end October, 1000–1300 & 1400–1700

Admission charges: Adult £1.50, child 75p

Facilities: Owned by National Trust. Inaccessible for coaches, small carpark. Shop. Visitors may picnic in garden. May be refreshments in 1988

Facilities for disabled: Access difficult (steps)

Collection: Models and half models of local vessels. Salcombe had strong connection in 19th century with schooners in the fruit trade. Model and album of *Herzogin Cecilie*. Photographs and paintings of locally built ships and wrecks. Paintings and ephemera.

St Ives Museum

Wheal Dream, St Ives, Cornwall
Telephone: 0736 796005

Location: In St Ives harbour area

Open: Monday to Saturday, daily 1000–1700, occasional Sundays

Admission charges: Adult 30p, child 10p

Facilities: Shop

Facilities for disabled: Access

Collection: Hain Room: models and mementoes of Hain Steamship Co, established in St Ives by Edward Hain, 1878, bought by P&O in 1917, phased out 1974. Clockwork from

Pendeen Lighthouse. Gibson photographs of Cornish wrecks. Fishing section with Pilchard Press.

Science Museum: *see* LONDON

Shamrock: *see* COTEHELE

SITTINGBOURNE

Dolphin Sailing Barge Museum

Crown Quay Lane, Sittingbourne, Kent
Telephone: 0622 62531

Location: From Sittingbourne High St turn at Cinema into Crown Quay Lane, opposite White Hart Pub turn into private road, Yard is off left of this

Open: Easter to October, Sunday and Bank Holidays 1100–1700

Admission charges: Run by Trust, details of membership and special arrangements for school visits from the Secretary, 117 Plains Avenue, Maidstone, Kent ME15 7AR

Facilities: Souvenir and book shop

Facilities for disabled: Housed in former sail loft, maritime material on ground floor, no special access

Collection: Museum occupies former barge-building and repair yard of Charles Burley Ltd, active 1880s–1965. Dolphin Sailing Barge Museum Trust formed 1969, after repair to buildings and dredging of silted inlet, the museum opened to public in 1970. Displays in former sail loft: ground floor, photographs, models, shipwrights tools and shop; upper floor: local industrial history. Forge opposite has old barge tillers used to support roof; barge ironwork displayed. Steam chest and boiler for plank shaping. Barge repairs carried out at the yard. Barges moored are private and not open to public, actively sailed and therefore coming and going.

Maritime Trust Thames barge *Cambria* (1906) moored here; in 1971 last cargo vessel working under sail alone on British Register, undergoing refit.

SOUTHAMPTON

Southampton Hall of Aviation

Albert Rd South, Royal Crescent, Southampton, Hampshire SO1 1FR
Telephone: 0703 35830

Location: Close to River Itchen, frequent buses from city centre

Open: Tuesday to Saturday 1000–1700, Sunday and Monday 1200–1700, Mondays in school holidays 1000–1700

Admission charges: Adult £1.40, OAP £1, child 70p. Reduced rates for groups of 12

Facilities: Shop and cafeteria

Facilities for disabled: Access. Lift

Collection: Solent was an important aviation centre 1909–1950s. Displays on local design and construction of seaplanes and flying boats. Includes; Supermarine S.6A (1929); Supermarine 228 Seagull; Supermarine 356 Spitfire F.24; Short S.25 Sandringham IV (Sunderland N158C III), built as Sunderland III (1943) converted to Sandringham IV (1947).

SOUTHAMPTON

Southampton Maritime Museum

The Wool House, Town Quay, Southampton, Hampshire
Correspondence Address: Southampton City Museums, Holyrood Chambers, 125 High St, Southampton
Telephone: Wool House 073 224216/332513. City Museums 0703 223941

Location: At the foot of High St and Bugle St, on Town Quay, south of the walled town

The tug tender *Galway Bay*, built in 1930 as *Calshot*, is being restored by Southampton City Museums. *R Bruce-Grice*

Open: Tuesday to Friday 1000-1300 & 1400-1700, Saturday 1000-1300 & 1400-1600, Sunday 1400-1700. Closed Monday and Bank Holidays

Admission charges: None

Facilities: Museum Education Service, details from Keeper of Museum Education

Facilities for disabled: Wheelchair access to 50% of museum

Collection: Museum will close in late 1988 and re-open at the Ocean Village, Princess Alexandra Dock, Southampton in early 1989. Themes to be main focus of new displays: Southampton, Gateway to the world (liners, cargo liners, ferries, excursion steamers etc. Passengers, mail and cargo); Working the Port (development and operational aspects of the Port of Southampton): Shipbuilding and repair (local maritime trades).

Tug tender *Calshot*, built Woolston, Southampton 1930. Not open to public, but access by arrangement

Sludge ship SS *Shieldhall* (1955), built Lobnitz and Co, Renfrew, being restored by SS *Shieldhall* Project, 48, Alexandra Rd, Shirley, Southampton. Currently at the Ocean Village, Princess Alexandra Dock.

SOUTHEND

Central Museum

Victoria Avenue, Southend-on-Sea, Essex SS2 6EX
Telephone: 0702 330214

Location: Turn right off A127 at roundabout into Victoria Avenue, Museum close to station

Open: Monday 1300-1700, Tuesday to Saturday 1000-1700

Admission charges: None

Facilities: Planetarium

Facilities for disabled: Wheelchair access at south entrance

Collection: Models, including Thames barges and bawleys, maritime artefacts. Local history and archaeology.

SOUTHPORT

Botanic Gardens Museum

Botanic Road, Churchtown, Southport PR9 7NB
Telephone: 0704 27547

Location: Situated on B5244, just off A565

Open: Tuesday to Saturday 1000-1800 April to October, 1000-1700 October to April, Sunday 1400-1700. Closed Monday except Bank Holidays, Friday following a Bank Holiday, Christmas Day, Boxing Day, New Year's Day and Good Friday

Admission charges: None

Facilities: Café, packed-lunch eating place nearby. School parties welcome by appointment; introductory talk possible. Loans of material to schools at Keeper's discretion. Gardens, fernery and aviary

Facilities for disabled: Ramp access to lower floor only

Collection: Displays change frequently. Logboat. Lifeboat and fishing boat models. Local shrimping industry.

Southsea

Royal Marines Museum

Curator Royal Marines Museum, RM Corps Secretariat, Royal Marines Eastney, Southsea, Hampshire PO4 9PX
Telephone: 0705 822351 ext 6134

Location: Eastern end of Southsea seafront, within Eastney Barracks

Open: Daily 1000–1630. Closed Christmas and Boxing Days.

Admission charges: Adult £1.50, OAP/child 70p. Concessions for group visits

Facilities: Educational visits welcomed and given special attention, with curatorial responsibility for accompanied tour around the museum. Heavy equipment displays in summer. Shop. Tea garden in summer

Facilities for disabled: Access limited due to stairs. Hands on exhibits

Collection: Housed in old Officers' Mess at RM Barracks. History of Marines from formation of Admiral's Regiment in 1664 to present. Static and audio-visual displays. Fine medal, uniform, picture and plate collections. Display on RM Band and allied Marine Corps. Equipment exhibition on lawns.

South Shields

South Shields Museum and Art Gallery

Ocean Rd, South Shields, Tyne and Wear NE 33 2TA
Telephone: 091 5141235

Location: In city centre on main street

Open: Weekdays 1000–1800, Sunday 1400–1700

Admission charges: None

Facilities: Shop and Cafeteria

Facilities for disabled: Ramp for access, lift to upper floors. Lavatory

Collection: Section in local history displays on maritime commerce and industry. Models and illustrations. The role of the town in lifesaving and lifeboat development.

Lifeboat *Tyne* (1833), withdrawn from service 1887, having assisted in saving 1024 lives. One of oldest lifeboats in existence. On the promenade.

Tugnet Icehouse

Tugnet, Spey Bay, Fochabers, Moray. Correspondence to
Falconer Museum, Tolbooth St, Forres, Moray IV36 0PH
Telephone: 0309 73701

Location: From A96 take B9104 from Fochabers to Spey Bay

Open: June to September, daily 1000–1600

Admission charges: None

Facilities: Parking. Sales point. Audio-visual show on request

Facilities for disabled: Access

Collection: Largest icehouse in Scotland, built 1830 to store ice
for packing salmon. Exhibition on salmon fishing industry
and wildlife of Spey estuary.

Stoke Bruerne, home of the
Waterways Museum, c1910,
showing the top lock and
corn mill which now houses
the museum exhibitions.
The Waterways Museum

The Waterways Museum

Stoke Bruerne, Towcester, Northamptonshire NN12 7SE
Telephone: 0604 862229

Location: By car: situated south of Northampton and
northeast of Towcester between M1, junction 15, and A5, just
off A508. By train: buses from Northampton and Wolverton
stations. By bus: information from United Counties, telephone
0604 36681

Open: Easter to October, daily 1000-1800. October to Easter
Tuesday to Sunday 1000-1600. Closed Mondays October to
Easter, Christmas Day, Boxing Day. Last admission 30
minutes before closing

Admission charges: Adult £1.20, OAP/child 60p, family (2
adults plus 3 children) £2.75. Special rates for parties by prior
arrangement

Facilities: Parking and shop

Facilities for disabled: Access restricted as housed on three
floors of old warehouse

Collection: Housed in cornmill, three floors of exhibitions.
Stoke Bruerne was a gathering place for boat people and the
museum illustrates two centuries of waterway life. Butty boat
cabin, painted wares. Contemporary prints, plans and
photographs. Boat weighing machine from the Glamorgan
Canal, Cardiff. Cast iron lock gates from Montgomery Canal
at Welshpool. Anderton lift. Blisworth Tunnel, longest still in
use on waterways system, a short walk along the tow path.

Tolbooth Museum

The Harbour, Stonehaven, Kincardineshire. Correspondence
to Peterhead Arbuthnot Museum (see above)
Telephone: 0779 77778

Location: A92, 94 or 957 into Stonehaven, museum on quay in
harbour

Open: 1 June to 30 September, Monday and Thursday to
Saturday 1000-1200 & 1400-1700, Wednesday, Sunday 1400-
1700. Closed: Tuesday

Admission charges: None

Facilities: Parking and shop

Facilities for disabled: Access to two of three rooms, third
easily viewed from doorway

Collection: Housed in one of town's oldest buildings.
Collections and displays reflect Stonehaven's maritime
history. Fishing boat models, including a Zulu. Fishing gear.
Ships in bottles.

Stromness Museum

Stromness, Orkney
Telephone: 0856 850025

Location: Ferry from Scrabster to Stromness or from Lerwick
or Aberdeen to Kirkwall and 964 to Stromness

Open: All year, Monday to Saturday 1100–1300 & 1330–1700,
Thursday 1100–1300. July to August 1030–1230 & 1330–1700

Admission charges: Adult 20p, child 5p, group rates

Facilities: Parking

Facilities for disabled: Partial access

Collection: Orkney and the sea, fishing, whaling,
boatbuilding. Ship models including steamer to sail between
Orkney and the mainland in 1856; schooner *Lavinia* (1859);
Great Eastern (1858) and the yole *Edith*. Lighthouse models.
Model trawler engines. Permanent feature on World War I and
scuttling of German Fleet at Scapa Flow. Hudson's Bay Co
display.

The Waterways Museum
collections illustrate
waterway life as well as
craft. *The Waterways
Museum*

Sunderland Museum and Art Gallery

Borough Rd, Sunderland SR1 1PP
Telephone: 091 514 1235

Location: At crossroads of A690, Holmeside Rd, and A1016, Burdon Rd. Close to BR and bus stations

Open: Tuesday to Friday 1000–1730, Saturday 1000–1600, Sunday 1400–1700

Admission charges: None

Facilities: Sales point. Education area for school and college parties. Quiz sheets. Loans to schools and colleges. Identification and advice service. Café (1000–1645 weekdays, 1000–1145 Saturday)

Facilities for disabled: Ramp and lift

Collection: Shipping displays concerned with the town's role in merchant ship building. Large collection of builders' models of sail, steam and motor vessels constructed on Wearside over last 150 years, particularly 19th-century Doxford Yard turret steamers. Important local maritime painting collection. Roker Lighthouse Optic (1903). Large model of Doxford Opposed Piston Marine Oil Engine (1951).

SWANSEA

Swansea Maritime and Industrial Museum

Museum Square, Maritime Quarter, Swansea SA1 1SN
Telephone: 0792 50351/470371

Location: In maritime quarter, on north quay of marina at mouth of River Tawe, close to shopping centre. Within walking distance of bus and train stations

Open: Daily 1030–1730. Closed Christmas Day, Boxing Day, New Year's Day

Admission charges: None

Facilities: Parking nearby, shop, refreshments in Marina. Education Officer can provide workshops and quizzes for children

Facilities for disabled: Housed in Victorian warehouse, restricted access

Collection: Local life and history. Steam tug *Canning*, lightship *Helwick*, beam trawler *Katie-Ann* can be boarded at pontoon, April to September.

T

The Grand Western Horseboat Company

The Wharf, Canal Hill, Tiverton, Devon EX16 4HX
Telephone: 0884 253345

Location: Tiverton reached by M5 or A38. Grand Western Canal signposted from town centre

Open: For details of public trips contact company at address above. Private charter available

Admission charges: Available from company

Facilities: Parking, refreshments, bar

Facilities for disabled: Special trips. Some accommodation on regular trips. Wheelchair access very difficult. No wheelchair access to lavatory

Company offers horsedrawn boat trips on canal. Vessels include *Hyades*, narrow beam boat, built 1935, and which worked on Grand Union Canal.

TOPSHAM

Topsham Museum

25 The Strand, Topsham EX3 0AX
Telephone: 039 287 3244

Location: On the A377, east bank of the Exe, museum in main street. From BR Station follow Holman Way to the Quay, turn left along the strand

Open: February to November, Monday, Wednesday and Saturday 1400-1700, Sundays in August and September

Admission charges: Adult, 50p, OAP/child 30p

Facilities: Special opening times may be arranged for school visits. Questionnaires available

Facilities for disabled: Wheelchair access to natural history displays only. Stair-lift to maritime and local history displays. Tea terrace. Lavatory

Collection: Situated in Holman House, with sail loft. The history of Topsham as a port, particularly period 1680-1720 when serge trade flourished with strong links with ports of Amsterdam and Rotterdam. Shipbuilding in Topsham; wooden sailing vessels from Napoleonic wars to 1880s; features on yards at Countess Wear and Topsham owned by Robert Davy and Daniel Bishop Davy and on John Bagwell Holman's yards including eleven half-models from Holman's Higher Yard. Ship models, tools, anchors, figureheads, paintings and photographs.

Torbay Aircraft Museum

Higher Blagdon, Paignton, Devon TQ3 3YG
Telephone: 0803 553540

Location: 1½ miles off A385 Paignton-Totnes road. Devon
General Bayline bus services. BR services to Paignton

Open: Low season 1000–1700, high season 1000–1800

Admission charges: Adult £2.50, OAP £2.00, child £1.50.
Parties of 20, Adult £2.00, OAP £1.50, child £1.00

Facilities: Parking, shop, licensed cafeteria, picnic bar. Kennel
for dogs which are not allowed on museum premises. Public
telephone

Facilities for disabled: Access to site, inevitably restricted
viewing of aircraft. Lavatories

Collection: Among the collection, planes with maritime
functions include: De Havilland Vampire XE995; Sea Venom
XG 629; Sea Hawk WM961; De Havilland Chipmunk WB 758;
Percival Proctor G-ANYP. Focke-Achgelis, Fa. 330 Bachstelze,
single-seat gyro kite carried by Class IX U-boats during World
War II for convoy spotting. Airborne lifeboat, wooden,
designed by Uffa Fox, used in later part of World War II.
Various aircraft wreck finds. Also period costume, 00 gauge
railway and gardens.

Valhalla Figurehead Collection

Tresco, Isles of Scilly. (Administered by National Maritime
Museum, Greenwich.) *See also* ISLES OF SCILLY
Telephone: 0720 22849

Location: Helicopter service from Penzance, boats between
islands. Situated in Tropical Gardens

Open: April to October daily 1000–1600

Admission charges: Admission to gardens includes Valhalla;
adult £2.50, child under 14 free

Facilities: Shop, café. Booklet on collection available here and
from National Maritime Museum (see above)

Facilities for disabled: Access

Collection: 30 figureheads salvaged from ships wrecked on
Scillies' coasts.

Valhalla Figurehead Collection: *see* TRESCO

Warrington Museum and Art Gallery

Bold St, Warrington, Cheshire WA1 1JG
Telephone: 0925 30550

Location: In town centre, A49 and A57 run close by. Both BR stations are within 5-10 minutes walk

Open: Monday to Friday 1000-1730, Saturday 1000-1700

Admission charges: None

Facilities: Sales point. Identification service. Frequent temporary exhibitions. Pre-booked parties welcome, book with education officer

Facilities for disabled: Access very limited, museum on first floor. Arrangements to use service lift can be made. Braille leaflet available

Collection: Items on display of interest: Backstaff, octant, quadrants (one marked 1751), 19th-century sextant, mariner's compasses including one *c*1730, Chinese mariner's compass, memorabilia of Bank Quay Iron Co shipbuilders, logboat remains (11th and 12th century), scale model of tugboat *Cadishead.*

HMS Warrior: *see* PORTSMOUTH

Watchet Market House Museum

Market St, Watchet, Somerset. (Correspondence to 7, Periton Court, Parkhouse Rd, Minehead TA24 8AE)
Telephone: 0643 7132

Location: M5, then A39 from Bridgwater junction or A358 from Taunton junction. Near harbour slipway

Open: Easter and mid-May to end September, daily 1030-1230, 1430-1630 & evening opening during July and August 1900-2100

Admission charges: Adult 10p, child 5p

Facilities: Parking. Sales point. Audio-visual with several local history programmes

Facilities for disabled: Difficult entrance (steps). Displays on ground floor

Collection: Housed in listed building. Maritime history of port of Watchet: models, figurehead, paintings and photographs of harbour and sailing vessels.

WESTON-SUPER-MARE

Woodspring Museum

Burlington Street, Weston-super-Mare, Avon, BS23 1PR
Telephone: 0934 21028

Location: In centre of Weston-super-Mare, ½-mile from
railway station.

Open: All year, Monday to Saturday 1000–1700 (closed 1300–
1400 November to February)

Admission: Free

Facilities: Refreshments, souvenior shop. Schoolroom
available.

Facilities for the disabled: Lavatory

Collection: Seaside holiday gallery of Victorian and
Edwardian eras. Display about local fishing with mud sled,
model nets. mud sled, model flatner (Weston fishing boat).

A flatner, *c*1880, off
Weston-Super-Mare. The
Woodspring Museum owns
one, though it is not
currently on show.
Woodspring Museum

Weymouth Museum

Westham Rd, Weymouth, Dorset DT4 8NF
Telephone: 0305 774246

Location: Two minutes walk from the King's Statue at the end
of the esplanade (A353)

Open: October to April, Monday to Saturday 1000-1300 &
1400-1700, May to September, Monday to Saturday 1000-1530
and Sunday 1030-1630

Admission charges: Adult 65p, OAP 30p, child/student/UB40
free

Facilities: School parties should book in advance. Quiz sheets
available. Schools loan service

Facilities for disabled: All displays on ground floor, two steps
to enter museum, wheelchairs welcome

Collection: Maritime room contains a lerret, shipwreck,
smuggling and other maritime exhibits. George III's bathing
machine. Mixed local history collection. Strong emphasis on
pictures, prints and photographs of Weymouth's past.

Whitby Museum

Pannett Park, Whitby, North Yorkshire YO21 1RE
Telephone: 0947 602908

Location: A171 to Whitby, close to centre

Open: 1 May to 30 September, weekdays 0930-1730, Sundays
1400-1700. 1 October to 30 April, Monday & Tuesday 1030-
1300, Wednesday to Saturday 1030-1600, Sunday 1400-1600

Admission charges: Adult 30p, child 15p, Adult accompanying
school party 15p

Facilities: School parties welcome, pre-booking necessary in
summer

Facilities for disabled: No special facilities, wheelchairs by
previous arrangement

Collection: Two wings devoted to maritime subjects. Captain
James Cook and the Scoresbys, their achievements and
connection with Whitby. Ship models (150), from earliest
times to steam; Whitby shipbuilding. Ship portraits. Displays
on Whitby lifeboats and cobles.

Whitehaven Museum and Art Gallery

Civic Hall, Lowther St, Whitehaven, Cumbria CA28 7SH
(temporary address)
Telephone: 0946 67575 ext 31

Location: In main street, part of Civic Hall

Open; Monday to Friday 0900-1800, Saturday 1000-1600.
Closed Sunday, Bank Holidays

Admission charges: None

Facilities: Parking. Access to photographic collection. Slide
loan service. Study facilities by arrangement. Information
sheets and publications on a range of maritime subjects

Facilities for disabled: Access

Collection: Emphasis on Whitehaven area and Borough of
Copeland. Shipping and mining heritage, geology,
archaeology industrial and social history.

Wick Heritage Centre

Bank Row, Wick, Caithness
Telephone: 0955 3385

Location: A9 or A882 to Wick. In town centre follow Bridge
Road to Bank Row

Open: June to September, Tuesday to Saturday 1000-1230 &
1400-1700, Sunday 1400-1700. Groups by arrangement

Admission charges: Adult £1.00, OAP/child 50p

Facilities: Sales point. Gardens and tea room

Facilities for disabled: Partial access. Lavatories

Collection: Award-winning exhibition on fishing industry and
domestic life of fishermen. Herring industry in particular.

Windermere Steamboat Museum

Rayrigg Rd, Windermere, Cumbria LA23 1BN
Telephone: 09662 5565

Location: Rayrigg Rd is the A592, museum on shore between
junction with A591 and Lake Rd

Open: Easter to October inclusive, daily 1000-1700

Admission charges: Adult £1.50, OAP £1.25, child 85p, family
£4. (includes parking)

Facilities: Parking. Groups arriving by coach should contact
curator in advance. Refreshments and shop. Lecture theatre

and education service. Steam launch trips. Majority of displays undercover

Facilities for disabled: Site designed for disabled access. Special facilities

Collection: Steamboats and other vintage craft. Sailing yacht (1780), hull in almost perfect condition. SL *Dolly*, (1850) salvaged from bed of Ullswater, oldest mechanically powered boat in the world, original machinery and hull timbers. SY *Esperance* (1869), built for HW Schneider, oldest boat on Lloyd's Register of Yachts, first twin screw steam yacht built. Salvaged from lake bed in 1941, Captain Flint's houseboat in *Swallows and Amazons* by Arthur Ransome. Ferry *Mary Anne* (c1870), used as ferry between Ferry Hotel and Ferry Nab, in occasional use until the 1940s. SS *Raven* (1871), former Furness Railway Co cargo ship carrying goods around

The interior of the Windermere Steamboat Museum, showing the vessels afloat in the boathouse. *Windermere Steamboat Museum*

lake. Salvaged from seabed 1955. *Rob Roy* canoe (c1880). Beatrix Potter's rowing boat (1890), type used on shallow lakes and tarns, salvaged from tarn bed at Sawrey. SL *Bat* (1891) built by Brockbanks, used in early radio control experiment 1904. SL *Lady Elizabeth* (1895), Lune Valley water tube boiler enabled steam to be raised from cold in 10 minutes, typical of small launches of the period. SL *Branksome* (1896), elegant and sumptuous Victorian steam launch, with embossed velvet upholstery carpets and marble fittings. Tea urn boils a gallon of water in 10 seconds. SL *Otto* (1896), built of steel and for speed, can do 18mph. Early motor boat (1898), early internal combustion engine. SL *Osprey* (1902), Sissons compound engine, daily cruises for museum visitors. SL *Water Viper* (1907). SL *Swallow* (1911), classic Windermere steam launch. Motor boat *Canfly*, powered by Rolls Royce engine of 1917 from RNAS Airship SST3. Yacht *Dawn* (1934). Bermudan rigged Windermere 17ft class yacht. Yacht *Mañana* (c1900), prototype Windermere 17ft yacht. Speedboat *Jane* (1938), Chris Craft Special Race boat, Motorboat of the Year 1938. Motorboat *Raae* (1938), family day boat. Seaplane Glider (1943), first glider to take off from water, 1943, developed from standard Falcon 2 Glider. Hydroplane Cookie (1962), Boat of the Show at 1963 Boat Show. Windermere exhibition includes history and life around lake from pre-Roman to modern times.

YELVERTON

Buckland Abbey

Nr Yelverton, Devon. (Correspondence to Plymouth Museum and Art Gallery, see above)
Telephone: 0752 668000 ext 4383

Location: To west off A386 between Crownhill and Yelverton, signed

Open: Easter to September, weekdays 1100–1800, Sundays 1400–1800. October to Easter, Wednesday, Saturday, Sunday 1400–1700

Admission charges: Adult £1.50, child 75p. Parties 20% discount

Facilities: Parking. Refreshments. New facilities to be provided include learning centre and better visitor facilities

Facilities for disabled: Limited access. Renovations and modifications in progress to improve disabled facilities

Collection: 13th-century Cistercian Abbey, converted by Sir Richard Grenville, later owned by Sir Francis Drake. Now owned by National Trust. Under reorganisation. Ship models and Drake's Drum, Drake memorabilia.

Fleet Air Arm Museum

Royal Naval Air Station, Yeovilton, Ilchester, Somerset BA22 8HT
Telephone: 0935 840565

Location: 2 miles east of Ilchester on B315, off A303

Open: March to October 1000–1730. November to February 1000–1630. Closed Christmas Eve and Christmas Day

Admission charges: Adult £2.50, OAP £1.50, child £1.25

Facilities: Parking. Licensed restaurant, picnic area, shop and children's play area

Facilities for disabled: Good access to nearly all of museum. Parking. Catering. Lavatories. Concorde and shop not accessible

Collection: History of Naval Flying since 1908, on active airfield. Over 50 aircraft of Royal Naval Air Service and Fleet Air Arm including: replicas of World War I RNAS planes (airworthy); Swordfish and exhibition; Barracuda remains; Firefly FR4; Gannets, standard and AEW versions; Buccaneers (one pre-production): Tiger Moth; Sea Vampire (prototype which made first carrier landing, 1945); Walrus; Seafire; Scimitars. Concorde 002. Exhibitions on WRNS, Falklands Campaign, Kamikaze bombers.